& St Petersburg

Text by Neil Wilson
Updated by John Varoli
Managing Editor: Tony Halliday

Berlitz® POCKET GUIDE

Moscow

Eleventh Edition 2004

PHOTOGRAPHY
AKG London (page 19); Tom Le Bas (32, 36); Anna Mockford and Nick Bonnetti (3, 6, 10, 11, 18, 21, 22, 62, 64, 65, 69, 70, 71, 73, 74, 76, 80, 82, 85, 87, 93); Jon Spaull (4, 12, 26, 31, 34, 40, 41, 45, 48, 49, 50, 51, 53, 55, 57, 58, 59, 60); Topham Picturepoint (5, 8, 17, 38, 39, 42, 91); Neil Wilson (13, 33, 35, 43, 54, 56, 83, 96)
Cover picture by Harald Sund/Gettyimages

CONTACTING THE EDITORS
Every effort has been made to provide accurate information in this publication, but changes are inevitable. The publisher cannot be responsible for any resulting loss, inconvenience or injury. We would appreciate it if readers would call our attention to any errors or outdated information by contacting Berlitz Publishing, PO Box 7910, London SE1 1WE, England.
Fax: (44) 20 7403 0290;
e-mail: berlitz@apaguide.co.uk
www.berlitzpublishing.com

The Hermitage (page 65), one of the world's great museums known for its priceless art collections

St Peter and Paul Fortress (page 74), where Peter the Great began building St Petersburg

The glorious multi-domed St Basil's Cathedral (page 37) is perhaps the most famous sight in all Russia

TOP TEN ATTRACTIONS

The Bolshoi Theatre (page 40) for an unforgettable night at the opera or ballet

The Russian Museum (page 71) with its magnificent collection of Russian art from down the ages

◄

➤

The Kremlin (page 26), the living monument to Russian history, architecture and political power

Peterhof (page 77), the opulent summer residence of Peter the Great, complete with cascade and fountains

▼

➤

Kolomenskoe (page 56), erstwhile royal retreat now preserved as an architectural museum

St Isaac's page 68), one of the largest cathedrals in the world

➤

Lenin still draws the crowds to his mausoleum (page 38)

➤

CONTENTS

Fact Sheets

INTRODUCTION

Winston Churchill once famously described Russia as 'a riddle wrapped in a mystery inside an enigma'. For many visitors from the West, the mystery persists, despite the fall of the oppressive and secretive Soviet regime and the new era of 'openness' in Russian society. It is the riddle of a country caught between East and West, a modern, technological society deeply rooted in its peasant past. Moscow and St Petersburg—capitals present and past—are Russia's two great cities, and their story is the story of Russia. The differences between them reflect the different pressures which have been brought to bear on Russia—a country spanning 11 time zones that stretch from the Baltic Sea to the Bering Strait—throughout its long and turbulent past.

Moscow, the modern capital, occupies a central position in all aspects of Russian life— historical, political, economic, cultural and spiritual. Lying at the heart of the densely populated Russian plain, it forms the historical nucleus of the Russian empire and houses the present government; it is Russia's largest city, with a population of 11 million, an industrial powerhouse in the middle of the country's most developed region. The capital forms the spiritual and cultural heart of this vast nation, as both the seat of the Russian Orthodox Church and a precious repository of Russian art and architecture. Tolstoy wrote in *War and Peace* that every Russian regards Moscow as if she were his own mother.

Indeed, the tourist groups thronging Red Square are as likely to have come from Vladivostok or Novosibirsk as from London or New York. From East and West alike, they have

The Catherine Palace at Pushkin near St Petersburg.

Chatting on a Moscow street.

come to step inside the crenellated walls of the Kremlin, for so long the symbol of Soviet power – 24 hectares (60 acres) of history, art and architecture that alone would make Moscow one of the world's great tourist attractions. But the city beyond the walls has other delights in store for the traveller: splendid churches and cathedrals, magnificent museums and art galleries, and world-class performances of opera and ballet.

Behind the façades of the great boulevards and avenues lie the crooked, leafy back-streets that are so beloved of Muscovites, and are dotted with little parks and churches, like displaced village greens in the heart of the urban metropolis.

If Moscow is a manifestation of the introspective aspect of the Russian soul, then its outward-looking counterpart is to be found around 700 km (440 miles) to the northwest. St Petersburg – Russia's capital for over 200 years, from 1712 to 1918 – was originally conceived as a symbolic break with Moscow, and with the past. Peter the Great's city on the Neva was intended to be his 'Window on the West', the new capital of a new Russia that would shrug off its peasant ancestry and take its place as a modern world power.

The break with Moscow was reflected in Baroque and Classical buildings designed by Western architects; in the carefully planned and regimented city layout; in the landscaped parks and palaces reminiscent of Versailles; and particularly in the geography of its site.

St Petersburg is a great Baltic Sea port looking towards the West, in close proximity to Finland and Sweden, linked to the outside world by its maritime trade routes. All this stands in stark contrast to Moscow's splendid isolation deep in the heart of Mother Russia. St Petersburg has always enjoyed a freer interchange of ideas with the West, and to this day the city feels more European than Moscow. In the friendly rivalry between the two, Petersburgers regard themselves as more sophisticated and cosmopolitan, and dismiss the capital as an overgrown village of bureaucrats and transplanted peasants.

What's in a Name?

Anyone who has read a Russian novel will know how a single character can be referred to by many different names, depending on who is talking to him. There is a strict etiquette about how to refer to people. Every Russian has three names—first name, patronymic, and family name. The patronymic refers to the person's father, like the Scottish 'Mac,' and Irish 'O.' For example, Mikhail Sergeyevich Gorbachev means Michael, son of Sergei.

As for the etiquette, a Russian stranger would address him simply as Mikhail Sergeyevich. Foreigners are encouraged to also use this, but they can get away with calling him simply, Mr Gorbachev. The titles Mr and Mrs do exist in Russian, but they are hardly ever used. Close friends would call Gorbachev by the diminutive, Misha.

Once home of tsars and tsarinas, the Winter Palace in St Petersburg now houses the Hermitage Museum.

In St Petersburg you can marvel at the grand palaces of the tsars and tsarinas, monuments to imperial splendour that were nearly destroyed by decades of revolution, war and communist neglect. St Petersburg escaped the plague of skyscrapers and concrete monstrosities that disfigure the centre of Moscow, and it still rates as one of the world's most beautiful cities. Colour enhances the grandiose architecture—walls of turquoise, duck-egg blue, yellow ochre and pastel pink, trimmed with white and gold, reflect the deliberate attempt to brighten a grey northern climate. It is a city of the arts, too – proud home of the Hermitage, one of the world's greatest art collections, and of the Mariinsky Theatre of Opera and Ballet (formerly the Kirov), which produced such performers as Nijinskiy and Nureyev.

But Moscow and St Petersburg—as different in character as Catherine the Great and Ivan the Terrible—share a way of life that may bewilder visitors from the West. The two cities are struggling in their efforts to cope with legacies of the Soviet system, while simultaneously attempting to come to terms with the new realities of liberalisation. The majority of the populace live in small apartments, although some reside in communal flats, but utility bills are much cheaper than in the West. While Russians suffered much in the two years after the 1998 crash, since President Vladimir Putin came to power in 2000, the country's economy has been extremely robust, in large part buoyed by high oil prices. This has made a handful of Russians some of the richest people in the world, but the wealth is filtering down: Moscow and St Petersburg are now bustling cities where expensive foreign cars crowd the roads, and many locals go on spending sprees in fancy stores and pass their nights in fashionable clubs and cafés. True, the new prosperity mostly benefits the young, while those over 50 can barely eke out a living. But if you are fortunate enough to re ceive an invitation into a Russian home, you will be surprised at the magnificent spread on the table.

St Petersburg skyline.

Moscow and St Petersburg have always been intriguing and challenging destinations for travellers, and in these times of dramatic change, the challenge and intrigue are perhaps even greater. Cast aside your preconceptions and bring along an open mind and a sense of adventure – then you can begin to explore the heart of this vast enigma called Russia, and perhaps shed a little light on its mystery.

Cathedral of the Assumption in Moscow.

A BRIEF HISTORY

Early Moscow

The bristling towers of the Kremlin look down on the Moskva River from the crest of Borovitskiy (Pine Grove) Hill. From the time nearly a thousand years ago when the pine trees were felled to build the first wooden palisade, the rulers of this hilltop have overseen the growth of an empire that, in the 20th century, became the world's largest country, covering one-sixth of the land area of the planet.

Moscow was first mentioned in a handwritten chronicle in 1147, during the reign of Yuri Dolgorukiy, Prince of Suzdal. Prince Yuri, dubbed *dolgorukiy,* or 'long-armed', because of his passion for snatching land from his rivals, built a fort on top of Borovitskiy Hill, an easily defended bluff nestled in the crook of the Neglinnaya and Moskva rivers, and is thus celebrated as the founder of the city of Moscow. His statue stands on Tverskaya Street, opposite Moscow's City Hall.

The walls of the Kremlin were built during the reign of Ivan the Great.

Although a relative newcomer compared with the ancient towns of Kiev, Smolensk and Novgorod, Moscow was perfectly situated to benefit from commerce, sitting at the crossroads of east–west and north–south trade routes. This strategic location was envied by the Tartars to the east; the 'Golden Horde' swept repeatedly across the steppe to trample and burn Moscow.

The Muscovite princes decided that collaboration with the enemy was likely to be more profitable than resistance, and their shameless capitulation assured Moscow's success at the expense of rival Russian cities. Chief collaborator was Grand Prince Ivan I (1325–1340), whose zealous tax-collecting in the name of his Mongol overlords earned him the nickname Kalita, or 'Moneybags'. Ivan Kalita shrewdly enticed the Metropolitan of the Russian Orthodox Church to reside in Moscow, thus consolidating religious with political and economic power. Merchants, noblemen and artisans

A 13th-century encampment of Tatars.

all flocked to the newly blessed city to enjoy the protection of the church and the recently extended city walls. But the Tartars' favouring of Moscow soon backfired, as the growing principality eclipsed the power of the Khans, and finally defeated them in war under the leadership of Ivan III, also called Ivan the Great (1462–1505).

With the fall of Constantinople to the Muslim Turks in 1453, followed by Ivan the Great's marriage to the niece of the last Byzantine emperor, Moscow proclaimed itself the 'Third Rome', the last bastion of Christianity against the heathen hordes of the East. Ivan the Great also oversaw the construction of the brick walls and towers of the Kremlin that still stand today, and he adopted the double-headed eagle of Byzantium as the emblem of his expanding dominion.

Ivan the Terrible

Moscow continued to grow, and concentric defensive walls were raised along the lines now followed by the Boulevard Ring and Garden Ring. By the middle of the 16th century, the population had ballooned to 100,000, making it one of Europe's largest cities. Meanwhile, around the Kremlin, some of Russia's greatest architectural feats were being undertaken. The man who inspired this dynamism was Ivan IV, who became better known as Ivan the Terrible.

Ivan IV (1533–1584) came to the throne at the age of three, and ruled for the next 51 years. At 17 he was crowned by the Metropolitan as Tsar, or Caesar, and thus became the first Russian ruler to claim an Imperial title. His reign was not exclusively terrible. He introduced Moscow's first printing press, encouraged artists and artisans, and triumphed over the Tartars at Kazan and Astrakhan, extending his empire southwards to the Caspian Sea. To celebrate this great victory, he commissioned St Basil's Cathedral.

In spite of his many and varied achievements, he is more often remembered as a bloodthirsty tyrant who founded Russia's first secret police, revelled in torture and bloodshed, and dealt with opposition by murdering his rivals. Towards the end of his life he killed his own son in a fit of wild rage, while he himself died of natural causes – an uncharacteristic end for those violent times.

Ivan's heir, Fyodor I, was, unfortunately, feeble-minded, and when he died in 1598, the dynasty that had ruled Moscow for 300 years died with him. The throne was assumed by Boris Godunov, Ivan's opportunist brother-in-law (1598–1605), whose tale of political intrigue is recounted in Mussorgsky's eponymous opera. After Godunov's death, political uncertainty and counterclaims to the throne ushered in the 'Time of Troubles', a black period for Russian history, marred by famine, civil war, peasant revolt, and Polish and Swedish invasions.

The Romanov Dynasty

In 1613 a national assembly was convened to elect a new tsar. The reluctant nominee was 16-year-old Mikhail Romanov, a young nobleman related by marriage to Ivan IV. This was the beginning of the Romanov dynasty, which was to rule Russia for the next three centuries. Of the 18 Romanov emperors and empresses, none had a greater impact on the country than Mikhail's great-grandson Peter the Great (1682–1725).

Tsar Peter I was a man with a vision of a new Russia, a world power that looked to the West. He was the first tsar to venture outside Muscovy, visiting Germany, Holland and England as a young man, and returning with his notebooks crammed full of the latest developments in industry, education, shipbuilding and military technology. Westernising his court back in Moscow, he told them what kinds of clothes to wear, and imposed a tax on those who refused to shave off their beards. He imported technical experts, began military academies and schools of navigation, built a navy, developed the mining and metal-forging industries, introduced factories producing paper, cotton, wool and silk, and reformed the currency, calendar and alphabet.

But Peter's reforms were unpopular with the mass of his subjects, aimed as they were at educating only the ruling classes, and harnessing the rest of the country's people and resources in the realisation of his military ambitions. To those who opposed him he was a cruel and ruthless autocrat. Peasants were taken from their fields and families to fight in his campaigns, and oppressive taxes levied to pay for them. Soldiers who plotted against him were tortured and executed, their mutilated bodies left swinging by the Kremlin walls for months, a grisly reminder of the price of disloyalty. He even had his own son imprisoned and then killed. The construction of his grand, Western-style capital city on the River Neva cost the lives of thousands of workers.

The Founding of St Petersburg

Much of Peter's energy went into waging the Great Northern War with Sweden, which then controlled all the lands around the Baltic Sea. In 1703 Peter's forces captured

Peter the Great.

enemy outposts near the mouth of the River Neva, and a few weeks later began building a fortress on an island in the river – the Peter and Paul Fortress, both the nucleus of St Petersburg and Russia's first outlet to the Baltic. In all, 20,000 labourers began the work of realising the tsar's dream of a great port and metropolis, his 'Window on the West'. Thousands dropped from exhaustion, starvation or disease, and it was said that the foundations of the city were the very bones of its builders. Peter invited foreign architects to design the palaces and gardens, and 40,000 more workers were pressed into service to build them. So much construction material was needed that the erection of stone buildings elsewhere in Russia was forbidden.

In 1712 the Imperial court moved north, and Peter proclaimed St Petersburg his new capital. Emphasising the break with Moscow and its old-fashioned traditions, he commissioned a radically un-Russian cathedral inside the walls of his island fortress. Instead of the clustered domes of traditional Orthodox churches, the Cathedral of Peter and Paul bears a single, slender spire, a golden needle reaching up towards the sky.

St Petersburg, Peter the Great's 'Window on the West.

Catherine the Great

Catherine the Great (1762–1796), the most famous empress in Russian history, began her reign 37 years after Peter's death. Catherine was a German princess whose prodigious love life – she is said to have enjoyed 20 favourites during her reign – often overshadowed her other achievements. A shrewd, intelligent woman, she oversaw the expansion of the Russian empire into Lithuania, eastern Poland, Belorussia, Ukraine and the Crimea, and the institution of a programme of town planning and rebuilding. She also built grand palaces in St Petersburg, and her private art collection was the basis of what would later be called the Hermitage Museum.

Catherine the Great.

Rather less to her credit, she clung to autocratic power and failed to relieve the oppression and exploitation of the serfs.

Catherine's capricious son Paul reigned for five years after her death. His heavy-handed and regressive policies set back Russian civilisation appreciably, and angered both the nobility and the peasants. When a rowdy band of conspirators invaded his palace in 1801 and murdered him in his own bedchamber, the populace was overjoyed.

The Road to Revolution

One of the plotters implicated in the assassination of Paul I was his own son, who inherited the throne as Alexander I (1801–1825). He reversed most of his father's repressive laws, abolished the secret police, and achieved international fame as the handsome tsar who defeated Napoleon in 1812.

France's *Grande Armée* of 600,000 men swept eastwards through Smolensk and met the Russian forces at Borodino, outside Moscow. After a hard-fought battle, the Russian generals surrendered Moscow to the French, and Napoleon rode unopposed through the Trinity Gate of the Kremlin on 3 September 1812. The city had been evacuated, however, and the French army took control of a ghost town. That night a great fire broke out and ravaged the city for six days, destroying 80 percent of its buildings. Denied the spoils of war and running short of food, Napoleon marched out of Moscow and into the frosty embrace of the Russian winter. The regrouped Russian army chased and harried the tattered French all the way to Paris, inflicting defeat after ignominious defeat. The 'Fatherland War', as it came to be known, inspired great patriotism, but also led to the import of political ideas that would lead eventually to revolution.

The first attempt at overthrowing the tsarist government came with the death of Alexander I in December 1825. In an uprising led by reformist officers in St Petersburg's Senate Square, rebel soldiers demanded the abolition of serfdom and the institution of a constitutional monarchy. But their nerve failed, and Tsar Nicholas I turned his cannon on the rebels and cleared the square. Following six months of interrogation, the five aristocratic leaders of the so-called 'Decembrists' were hanged in the Peter and Paul Fortress, and thus became martyrs for generations of Russian revolutionaries. To commemorate them, the square is now called Decembrists' Square (Площадь Декабристов – *ploshchad Dekabristov*).

Political discontent erupted again in January 1905, when 150,000 workers marched en masse to Palace Square to deliver a petition to the tsar. The crowd was fired upon by his troops, and thousands were killed or injured. 'Bloody Sunday' – as it became known – provoked a wave of demonstrations and insurrections (including the famous mutiny on the battleship *Potemkin*), and culminated in October and November in the streets of Moscow with barricades and fighting. The revolution was eventually put down, and the leaders of the St Petersburg 'Soviet' (workers' council) arrested. However, the seeds of change had been sown.

When Russia joined the Allies in World War I, patriots changed the name of the capital from the German-sounding St Petersburg to Petrograd; but Russian involvement in the Great War proved to be the final straw for the oppressed masses. Incompetent leadership, appalling casualties, food shortages and a mood of general hopelessness led to another wave of strikes and riots. In February 1917, a mass of protesting workers joined the Petrograd garrison in an

Revolutionary painting in St Petersburg's Artillery Museum.

A symbol of times past.

uprising that finally forced the abdication of the tsar. In his railway carriage, set in a siding in the ancient town of Pskov, a shocked and desolate Nicholas II signed away some 300 years of the Romanov dynasty.

The Soviet Era

Eight months later the ultimate revolution took place in Petrograd. On 24 October 1917, the Bolshevik leaders staged a near-bloodless coup, storming the Winter Palace and seizing power from the Provisional Government. Promising 'peace, land and bread' to the peasants and power to the workers, Vladimir Ilyich Lenin began to mould the world's first Communist state.

The new Soviet government moved to the Kremlin in 1918, and Moscow once again became the Russian capital. In the wake of the October Revolution, civil war between Bolsheviks, or Reds, and anti-Bolsheviks, or Whites, ravaged Russia. On the orders of the Kremlin, Nicholas and his family were executed, and the Red Army triumphed over the counter-revolutionaries. In 1922, the Communist Party's new Secretary General, Josef Stalin (1922–1953), forced the non-Russian Soviet republics into federation with the Russian Republic, thus creating the Union of Soviet Socialist Republics – USSR.

Following Lenin's death in 1924, Petrograd was renamed Leningrad in his honour, and Stalin began to tighten his stranglehold on Soviet power. A planned economy, collectivised agriculture and a crash programme of industrialisation saw control of the Party penetrate every corner of Soviet life. Dissenting voices were stilled by Stalin's secret police, forerunners of the KGB. In the Great Purge of the 1930s, millions were imprisoned, exiled or executed.

Millions more died during World War II, the 'Great Patriotic War' that claimed 15 to 20 million Soviet lives. Hitler's panzer divisions invaded on 22 June 1941, and advanced as far as the gates of Moscow before a Soviet counter-attack beat them back. The Russian winter sapped the German resolve, the Soviet army regrouped, and Hitler suffered his first defeat. Leningrad was less fortunate, though it too held firm. The Germans blockaded the city for 900 days, and almost a million citizens perished. Many more would have starved were it not for the 'Road of Life' supply route across Lake Ladoga.

The aftermath of World War II saw the USSR emerge as a world superpower, but Stalin's suspicion of his Western allies initiated the era of mutual distrust that came to be called the Cold War. After Stalin's death in 1953, the leadership of Nikita Khrushchev (1953–1964) denounced the evils of the Stalinist regime and ushered in a brief thaw in international relations. But Leonid Brezhnev's long reign (1964–1982), known in Russia as the 'stagnation', saw power concentrated once more

Revolutionising the Calendar

In February 1918, Lenin reformed the Russian calendar to bring it into line with the rest of Europe. The move from the Julian calendar (Old Style) to the Gregorian calendar (New Style), which had been in use throughout Europe since the mid-18th century, involved the loss of 13 days, so that 31 January 1918 (OS) was followed by 14 February (NS). This explains why the anniversary of the October Revolution, which took place on 25 October 1917 (OS), was always celebrated on 7 November (NS), and why the Russian Orthodox Church celebrates Christmas on 7 January.

in the hands of one man. Corruption, nepotism and repression returned, living standards fell and economic crisis loomed.

Perestroika and Beyond

The death of Brezhnev in 1982 marked the end of the 'old guard', a generation of Communist ideologues whose time was past. When Mikhail Gorbachev came to power in 1985, he instituted policies of *glasnost* (openness) and *perestroika* (restructuring), aimed at decentralising management of the economy, encouraging free enterprise and prising power out of the hands of the Communist Party. On 26 March 1989, the Soviet people voted in the first national election since 1917. Communist regimes throughout Eastern Europe toppled like dominoes, the Berlin Wall came down and the Baltic States declared independence.

In August 1991, Boris Yeltsin averted an attempted coup by Communist hard-liners and became a national hero. Bowing to popular opinion, Gorbachev resigned on 25 December 1991, and 70 years of Soviet rule came to an end. The USSR was dissolved and Yeltsin was elected President of the Russian Republic. The red flag that once flew above the Kremlin walls has been replaced with the white, blue and red stripes of Russia.

And so began a new age of restructuring the economy and reforming Russia's political system. As the country struggled to meet the challenges of democracy and the free market, the prevailing spirit was one of optimism. The country, however, suffered after the August 1998 financial crisis, and the outbreak in 1999 of a second war in Chechnya was a terrible trauma – not least for Chechen civilians. In 2000 Vladimir Putin, who had been elected prime minister of Russia in 1999, was made president of the federation. Today the Russian economy is growing and people are once again starting to believe in the future.

WHERE TO GO

MOSCOW

The city of Moscow lies deep in the heart of the Russian plains, in the wide, shallow valley of the Moskva River. A map of the city records its growth in a series of concentric circles, like the rings of a tree, centred on the ancient fortress of the Kremlin. The innermost ring, the 15th-century Kremlin wall, remains impressively intact, while the Boulevard Ring, a wooded avenue, curves around the line of the 16th-century city walls.

About 3km (2 miles) out from the Kremlin, the Garden Ring is a busy, multi-lane traffic artery, which follows the circular line of a 14½-km (9-mile) earthwork defence built at the end of the 16th century. The name itself dates from the 19th century, during which the rampart was replaced by a tree-lined boulevard, which is itself now sadly superseded by

Moscow's Metro Stations

There are few cities in the world where an underground railway system would rate as a tourist attraction, but in Moscow the Metro is a must. From street level, dizzily long escalators (the stations were designed to be used as bomb shelters) plunge down to stations ornamented with heroic sculptures, paintings, stained glass, carvings, mosaics and glittering chandeliers. Among the most splendid are Revolution Square, Mayakovskaya, Kropotkinskaya and Kievskaya. The cheap fare will secure you unlimited mileage on the fast and frequent trains. The Metro network, begun in 1935 and still being extended, mirrors the street layout, with radial lines linked by a circle line that roughly follows the Garden Ring.

the present traffic-clogged motorway. The outermost ring is the Moscow Ring Road, a 108-km (68-mile) motorway which marks the present-day city limits.

The Moskva River, a tributary of the Oka – which in turn flows into the mighty Volga – winds through the city in a series of wide and sweeping loops. Excursion boats ply back and forth among the barges and freighters, offering an interesting and relaxing introduction to the Russian capital. You can board one of these **boat trips** at the embarkation point beside the Kiev Railway Station (Киевский вокзал–*kievskij vokzal*), which is easily reached by Metro. The trips are good value, and last about an hour and a half. On the return trip you can get off the boat at the jetty by the Hotel Rossia, near Red Square, or at Gorky Park.

View over the Kremlin.

But where should you start seeing it all? Even if you have only a few hours to spare between flights, there is one essential trip which allows you to experience a living monument to Russian history, architecture and political power. It is, of course, the Kremlin (Кремль–*kreml'*).

The Kremlin

The Kremlin's main entrance is via the impressive **Trinity Tower** (Троицкие Ворота–*troitskie vorota*). Built in 1495, and at 80 metres (260 feet) the tallest of all the Kremlin towers, it is linked to the low, white Kutafya Tower by a bridge that once spanned the Neglinnaya River (the waters of which now flow through an underground tunnel). The deep cellars of the tower were designed as ammunition stores, and also served as dungeons during the 16th and 17th centuries. It was through the Trinity Gate that Napoleon's army entered the Kremlin in September 1812.

Once inside the walls, remember that the area to the left of the gate is out-of-bounds to the public. If you stray too far, the Kremlin guards will shepherd you back onto the pavement. The buildings here, in the northern part of the citadel, handsomely painted with yellow walls, green roofs and white trim, include the **Arsenal**, the **Senate**, with its domed roof, and the **Presidium of the Supreme Soviet**, now the seat of Russian government. On the right is the **Palace of Congresses** (Кремлёвский дворец съездов–*Kremlyovskij Dvorets Sjezdov*), a monolith of white marble and glass built in 1961. Its 6,000-seat auditorium once hosted Communist Party meetings, but is now the gathering place of the Congress of People's Deputies. The palace is also open to the public as a concert hall and opera venue.

Opposite the Senate building is the huge **Tsar Cannon** (Царь-пушка–*tsar'-pushka*), a masterpiece of Russian metal-casting and one of the biggest cannons ever produced. Made in 1586, ornately filigreed and decorated with a portrait of Tsar Fyodor I (son of Ivan the Terrible), it was probably never fired in anger. Past the cannon is the entrance to **Cathedral Square**, which, in addition to being the most historic part of the Kremlin, is also a significant monument to Russian religious art and architecture.

On the right, behind the Tsar Cannon, is the **Cathedral of the 12 Apostles** (собор Двенадцати апостолов–*sobor*

dvenadsati apostolov), with its five silver domes, and the
Patriarch's Palace (Патриаршие палаты—*patriarshye
palaty)*, which was the home of the spiritual leader of the
Russian Orthodox church in the 17th century and had apartments for both private and ceremonial use. Together these
two buildings house over 700 items comprising a museum of

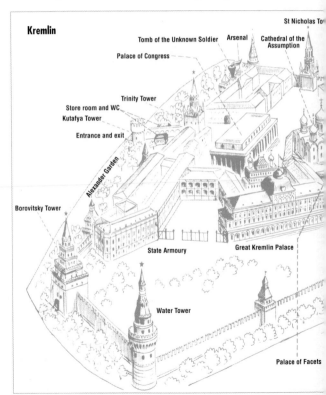

Kremlin

St Nicholas To…
Tomb of the Unknown Soldier
Arsenal
Cathedral of the Assumption
Palace of Congress
Trinity Tower
Store room and WC
Kutafya Tower
Entrance and exit
Alexander Garden
Borovitsky Tower
State Armoury
Great Kremlin Palace
Water Tower
Palace of Facets

17th-century applied art, including decorated Bibles, books, jewellery, embroidery, cutlery and furniture.

Ahead, in the middle of the square, stands the massive **Cathedral of the Assumption** (Успенский собор – *uspenskij sobor*), with painted semi-circular gables and five golden domes. Built between 1475 and 1479 by the Italian architect

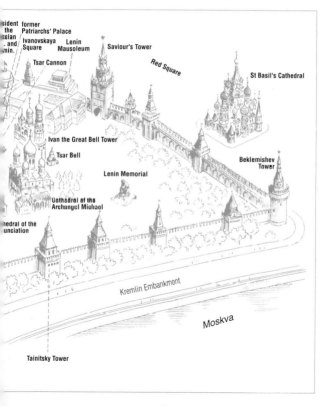

29

Aristotle Fioravanti of Bologna, the cathedral was used for the coronations of Russia's rulers. The interior is richly decorated with frescoes and icons, most notably the famous *Holy Virgin of Vladimir* on the iconostasis. This is a 15th-century copy of the 12th-century Byzantine original, which is now housed in the Tretyakov Gallery. Although the cathedral was ransacked during the retreat of Napoleon's troops in 1812, some of the five tons of looted silver was recovered. This was later used to make the main chandelier when restoration work was being carried out.

Tucked behind the cathedral is the small white **Church of the Deposition of the Robe** (церковь Ризположения – *tserkov' rizpolozheniya*), a single-domed church dating from the late 15th century. Inside walls, pillars and arches are all covered with beautiful frescoes dating from 1644, which have been restored to their original brilliance. The cluster of 11 golden cupolas beyond belongs to the Terem Palace (closed to the public).

The faceted stone wall overlooking the square belongs to the **Palace of Facets** (Грановитая палата – *granovi-*

What's an Iconostasis?

In a Russian Orthodox church, the iconostasis is a high partition that separates the main part of the church from the sanctuary, at the back. It is decorated with painted wooden panels of religious images, or icons, which are arranged in a set order around the door in the centre, through which the priest emerges to administer the Eucharist. The Virgin and Child are to the left of the doorway; to the right is Christ Pantocrator (Christ in Majesty – the Second Coming), while above are scenes from the lives of biblical figures and representations both of the Twelve Apostles and the Archangels Michael and Gabriel.

The Cathedral of the Annunciation.

taya palata), one of the oldest official buildings in Moscow (built 1487–1491). The Italian architects Marco Rufo and Pietro Solario created a vast, magnificent hall with a vaulted ceiling balanced on a single, central pillar, lavishly decorated in its entirety with colourful murals (closed to the public).

The **Cathedral of the Annunciation** (Благов-ещенский собор – *blagoveshchenskij sobor*), with nine gilded onion domes, is to the left of the palace. The three central cupolas date from the 15th century, and six more were added during the 16th. This was the Chapel Royal, the private church of the tsars, where they were christened and married. The interior has a floor of warm, red-brown jasper, and a magnificent iconostasis with priceless icons by the master Andrei Rublev and his teacher Theophanes the Greek. Ivan the Terrible had to build his own entrance and screened chapel here, for he was barred from using the main entrance by the church authorities after his fourth marriage in 1572.

Christened in the Cathedral of the Annunciation, and then crowned in the Cathedral of the Assumption, Russian tsars were buried in the **Cathedral of the Archangel Michael** (Архангельский собор—*arkhangel'skij sobor*). It was built between 1505 and 1508 in a blend of Russian and Italian styles, and dedicated to the Archangel Michael, the traditional guardian angel of the princes of Moscow. Inside, the 46 tombs are the last resting places of princes, tsars and a range of Imperial dignitaries, from Ivan Kalita (d. 1341) to Ivan V (d. 1696), including the remains of Ivan the Terrible. During restoration work in the 1950s, murals dating back to the late 17th century were discovered behind layers of dirt and dust. The most impressive work of art is a 14th- or 15th-century icon of the Archangel Michael, which is located on the right-hand side of the door in the iconostasis.

Soaring gracefully above Cathedral Square is **Ivan the Great's Bell Tower**

Ivan the Great's Bell Tower houses 21 bells, the largest of them weighing in at 64 tons.

(колокольня Ивана Великого – *kolokol'nya ivana velikogo*). The lower part was built in the early 1500s as a church and watch-tower; then in 1600 Boris Godunov had it raised to its present height of 81 metres (265 feet), so allowing the tsar's look-outs to scan the horizon up to 32 km (20 miles) away. Its golden onion dome remains one of the city's most distinctive landmarks.

The Tsar Bell, at 200 tons, is the largest in the world – though it was cracked before it was ever rung.

Weighing in at 64 tons, the biggest of the 21 bells is housed in the shorter, neighbouring tower, dwarfing even London's Big Ben, which clocks up a mere 13½ tons. But even these are toys compared to the massive **Tsar Bell** (Царь-колокол – *tsar'-kolokol*), a 200-ton giant that is undisputedly the largest bell in the world. The skilled father-and-son team of master craftsmen, Ivan and Mikhail Motorin, took two years to cast the bell between 1733 and 1735, but disaster struck before it had been removed from the casting pit. A great fire swept through the Kremlin, and when well-meaning firefighters deluged the still-hot bell with water, it cracked. The 11-ton chunk that split off now stands at the foot of the bell tower, propped up beside the rest of the delicately decorated monster.

At the far end of Cathedral Square, under the huge façade of the **Great Kremlin Palace** (Большой кремлёвский дворец–*bol'shoy kremlyovskiy dvorets*; closed to the public), which overlooks the river, turn right and then proceed downhill to the **Armoury** (Оружейная палата–*oruzhejnaya palata*). It's best to take a guided tour around this treasure house exhibiting the crowns, jewels, robes and thrones of the tsars.

This building, which was once the home of the Imperial gold- and silversmiths, now houses the oldest museum in Russia, crammed with the riches accumulated by state and church over many centuries. Here you can see Ivan the Terrible's throne; the Monomakh Crown, which graced the heads of Russia's rulers in the 16th and 17th centuries; the sumptuous wedding gown of Catherine the Great; and the coach in which she travelled from St Petersburg to Moscow for her coronation. Also exhibited are the 14th-century vestments of Peter, the first Metropolitan of Moscow; Boris Godunov's armour; and a display of Fabergé jewellery, including a number of the world-renowned eggs that were made for the tsar every Easter.

Cannon at the Armoury.

A separate guided tour can be organised to see the neighbouring **Diamond Exhibition**, which has among its plethora of gems the 190-

*The Tomb of the Unknown Soldier – 'Your name is
unknown, your deeds immortal'.*

carat diamond received by Catherine the Great from her
lover Grigory Orlov.

Leave by the **Borovitskaie Gate**, and you will find yourself
in the **Alexander Gardens** (Александровский сад–*alek-
sandrovskij sad*), a leafy glade running along the west wall
of the Kremlin, named after Tsar Alexander I. At the northern end, beneath the spire of the Corner Arsenal Tower, lies
the **Tomb of the Unknown Soldier,** which is dedicated to
the memory of those who fell while defending the city from
Hitler's invasion in the Battle of Moscow in 1941. 'Your
name is unknown, your deeds immortal', reads the poignant
inscription. This is a popular spot with newlywed couples,
who often come to lay flowers on the tomb and have their
picture taken beside the eternal flame.

Red Square

East of the Kremlin lies **Red Square** (Красная площадь–*krasnaya ploshchad'*), the giant parade-ground where, every 1 May and 7 November, the massed military might of the Soviet Union marched beneath the inscrutable gaze of the Politburo. At the far end of the square, rising high above the cobblestones, are the improbable towers of **St Basil's Cathedral** (собор Василия Блаженного–*sobor vasiliya blazhennogo*) may be the most famous sight in all of Russia. Originally called the Cathedral of the Virgin of the Intercession, this architectural fantasia of multi-coloured onion domes was raised by Ivan the Terrible in 1555–1561 in thanks for his victory over the Tartars in 1552. Legend has it that Ivan put out the eyes of the architect, for fear that he might build a more beautiful church elsewhere. Although some visitors find the interior rather an anticlimax, the eight chapels set around the central church do contain colourful frescoes. An extra chapel was added in 1588 to house the remains of St Basil the Blessed – the holy fool – whose name soon became synonymous with the whole cathedral.

The bronze statue in front of St Basil's is of **Minin and Pozharsky,** the two heroes whose brave leadership saved the city from the Polish invasion in the Time of Troubles. The raised circular platform nearby is the **Lobnoye Mesto** (Лобное место), or Place of Skulls, where imperial decrees were announced.

Watch out for black limousines swishing in and out of the **Saviour Gate,** carrying high-ranking government officials to and from the Kremlin. The elegant 67-metre (220-foot) **Saviour Tower** (Спасская башня–*spasskaya bashnya*), above the gate, houses a belfry, which chimes out the quarter hours.

Opposite: St Basil's Cathedral

Lenin in his mausoleum – still a major attraction, both for Russians and foreigners.

The **Lenin Mausoleum** (Мавзолей Ленина—*mavzolej lenina*), a low, stepped pyramid in red and black Ural granite, attracts long queues of pilgrims who wait for hours to see the embalmed body of the founder of the Soviet Union. (An Intourist guided tour will let you jump the queue.) When the Lenin Mausoleum is open, most of Red Square is closed to the public.

After descending to the funeral hall, you emerge at the side of the mausoleum and can, if you choose, walk the length of the Kremlin Wall to view the last resting places of heroes of the State, including Josef Stalin, cosmonaut Yuri Gagarin and American John Reed, author of *Ten Days that Shook the World.* You will look in vain for the name of Nikita Khrushchev, however, for the leader who attempted to lift the oppressive legacy of the Stalin years died in political disgrace in 1971, and was denied a place in this hallowed spot. His grave lies in the cemetery of the Novodevichij Convent (see pages 50–1).

The ornate façade across Red Square and facing the museum belongs to the famous Department Store, otherwise known by its memorable Russian acronym **GUM** (ГУМ)  (Государственный универсальный магазин–*gosudarstvennyj universal'nyj magazin*). Built in the late 19th century, three parallel, glass-roofed arcades house three floors of shops and an ornamental fountain. These days the store is divided into small shops, many of which feature well-known Western brand names, and it is now possible to purchase almost everything you could want, from televisions and camcorders to Paris fashions and perfumes.

The area of narrow streets and old buildings to the rear of GUM is known as **Kitai-gorod,** and once served as the city's merchant district. *Kitai-gorod* translates as 'Chinatown', though you won't see crowds of Chinese here; the name probably derives from the Old Russian word *kiti*, meaning 'palisade'.

The GUM department store on Red Square.

Closing off the north end of the square is the red-brick bulk of the **History Museum** (Исторический музей) – *istoricheskij muzey*), which opened in 2000 after a long renovation. Exhibits of coins, costumes, ancient tools and weapons, as well as various ornaments, illustrate the evolution of the many and diverse peoples inhabiting the territory of the former Soviet Union.

Other Central Squares

The huge, traffic-clogged expanse beyond the History Museum is Manezhnaya Square, flanked by the Classical Central Exhibition Hall, the turn-of-the-century National Hotel, and the vast, forbidding, grey walls of the Hotel Moskva. One block east and far more appealing, **Theatre Square** (Театральная площадь–*teatral'naya ploshchad'*) is dominated by the pink-and-white, wedding-cake façade of the world-famous **Bolshoi Theatre** (Большой театр–*bol'shoy teatr*), built in the 1850s to replace the original theatre of 1824, which had burnt down. The Classical portico, crowned by a bronze sculpture of Apollo's chariot drawn by four prancing steeds, leads to an auditorium draped in so much red and gold that it is almost sinfully sumptuous. Tchaikovsky's *Swan Lake* premiered here in 1877, and still plays each year to packed houses. No visit to Moscow is complete without a night at the opera or ballet. Bear in mind that the Bolshoi is in the midst of a major restoration, and the old stage is sometimes closed. You must check with the theatre for more precise information.

At work on the Bolshoi.

A new and modern Bolshoi theatre stage, however, opened in 2002 just next to the old theatre, and performances continue there without any interruption. Winter is the best time to catch the leading artists, as they are often on tour abroad during the summer. No matter who's on stage, a visit to the Bolshoi is an unforgettable experience.

Bolshoi ballerina.

Opposite the Art-Nouveau façade of the **Metropol Hotel**, the garden in the centre of the square shades a statue of Karl Marx – the father of Communism – which is inscribed with the exhortation 'Workers of the world, unite!' Another Communist hero is celebrated in the **Central Lenin Museum** (Центральный музей Ленина–*tsentral'nyj muzej Lenina*), the red-brick former town hall on the south side of the square. However, much of the Lenin paraphernalia has been packed away and only a few rooms are now dedicated to the revolutionary leader, with most of the museum used as a space for other exhibitions. Looking more than a little incongruous among all the Communist propaganda is the Soviet leader's personal Rolls-Royce Silver Ghost.

The museum is located next to **Revolution Square** (Площадь революции–*ploshchad' revol'utsii*), the scene of fierce street-fighting during the October Revolution in 1917. The ordinary people who gave their lives in the battle are remembered in the splendid bronze sculptures that grace the platform in the adjacent **Metro** station.

From Karl Marx's statue, the view right, up Teatral'niy Proyezd, is blocked by the vast bulk of the **Lubyanka** building – a notorious yellow edifice, the headquarters of the once-dreaded KGB (*Komitet Gosudarstvennoj Bezopasnosti* – Committee for State Security). Countless thousands of political prisoners disappeared into its basement dungeons, never to be seen again. A statue of Felix Dzerzhinsky, founder of the Cheka, the Soviet state's original secret police, stood in the middle of the square facing the Lubyanka. With the fall of Communism, rejoicing crowds saw the hated figure toppled in August 1991. In the nearby park, a new, small stone monument remembers the millions who suffered and died in the purges of the Stalin era.

Cool couple on Tverskaya Street.

Bustling **Tverskaya Street** (улица Тверская–*ulitsa Tverskaya*) is Moscow's main shopping street, and a sign of changing times is the number of familiar and decidedly non-communist, names springing up along its sidewalks, including Benetton, Yves Rocher, Pizza Hut and McDonald's, among others. In between are other shops. Look out for the **Yeliseyevsky Store**, an or-

Strolling off the Boulevard Ring.

nate and lavishly chandeliered pre-revolutionary food shop which has since been preserved in its original condition.

At the top of the hill is Tverskaya Square, with the Moscow City Hall on the left, facing a statue of Prince Yuri Dolgorukiy, the city's founder. Close by is **Pushkin Square** (Пушкинская площадь – *Pushkinskaya ploshchad'*), a Russian Piccadilly Circus at the intersection of Tverskaya Street and the Boulevard Ring, complete with the country's first McDonald's restaurant, thronging with trendy young Muscovites and lit by a neon Coca Cola sign flashing from the roof-tops.

Around the Boulevard Ring

Following the line of an old city wall is the **Boulevard Ring** (Бульварное кольцо – *bul'varnoye kol'tso*), a circular boulevard which, for the better part of its length, has a pleasant, wooded park down the middle, with statues, old iron benches and lamp-posts, as well as playgrounds for the children. Fine old 19th-century buildings line its sides.

Southwest of the Kremlin and inside the Boulevard Ring is the Classical white marble façade of the **Pushkin Museum of Fine Arts** (Музей изобразительних искусств имени Пушкина — *muzej izobrazitel'nykh iskusstv imeni Pushkina*). Dedicated to the history of world art, the collection of painting and sculpture ranges from antiquity to the 20th century.

Highlights include works by Rembrandt, Rubens and Van Gogh, as well as an extremely impressive collection of 19th- and 20th-century French art — Cézanne, Corot, Degas, Gauguin, Manet, Monet, Picasso, Matisse, Renoir and Toulouse-Lautrec are all here, to name only the top ten. Russian collectors were among the first to appreciate such artists.

Fallen Heroes

During the Soviet era, many cities, streets and squares were renamed after famous revolutionaries and leading figures in the Communist Party. Statues and monuments were raised in their honour — Lenin, Kalinin (Chairman of the Presidium of the Supreme Soviet, 1919–1946), Sverdlov (first Soviet head of state), Dzerzhinsky (founder of the Cheka secret police), Kirov (assassinated leader of the Leningrad Party organisation), Gorky (revolutionary author) and others were celebrated in this way.

With the fall of the Communist Party, the statues, now seen as reminders of a hated and oppressive regime, were toppled, and many place names have reverted to their pre-revolutionary forms. Thus Leningrad is once again St Petersburg, and Moscow's Gorky Street and Sverdlov Square have reverted to their former titles of Tverskaya Street and Theatre Square.

Just across the street is the new **Cathedral of Christ the Saviour**, originally built between 1839 and 1883 as a monument to the 1812 war with Napoleon. This vast – it could hold a congregation of 10,000 – and beautiful church was dynamited in 1931 in an incredible act of cultural vandalism, to make way for a planned Palace of Soviets. The palace was originally intended to be the world's largest building, crowned by a 100-metre (330-foot) statue of Lenin, a symbol of Soviet achieve-

The Pushkin Museum of Fine Arts.

ment. It was never built, and the hole in the ground became a gigantic, circular, open-air swimming pool, which was for many years a Moscow landmark. Now the swimming baths have gone in their turn, and reconstruction of the Cathedral of Christ the Saviour was completed in 1997, in time for Moscow's 850th anniversary.

Just a few blocks away is the **Alexander Pushkin Museum** (Музей Пушкина –*muzej Pushkina*), which ought not to be mixed up with the other Pushkin Museum – of Fine Arts. The two institutions have nothing in common except the name of Russia's most famous poet and the Classical columns of their façades. This Pushkin Museum celebrates the career of the much-revered poet, and houses a collection of his manuscripts and personal possessions. Although he himself never lived here, the building – a stuccoed timber classic from 1814 – is of architectural interest.

In addition to Pushkin, several other Russian literary figures are honoured in widely dispersed museums of varying significance. Fans can choose from the Chekhov (Музей

Russian Writers

World literature acknowledges a major debt to the Russian writers of the 19th century. The four famous names that follow are commemorated in their own Moscow museums.

ALEKSANDR SERGEEVICH PUSHKIN (1799–1837) is the undisputed national genius, credited with founding modern Russian literature. Every Russian schoolchild can quote, with pride, verse after verse of Pushkin's poetry. His major works include the verse novel *Eugene Onegin*, the romantic poems *Ruslan and Lyudmila* and *The Prisoner of the Caucasus*, and the historical tragedy *Boris Godunov*.

FYODOR MIKHAILOVICH DOSTOEVSKY (1821–1881) once faced the tsar's firing squad, but was spared at the last moment and exiled to Siberia instead. The great novelist later wrote about these experiences in *The House of the Dead*. His psychological novels *Crime and Punishment* and *The Brothers Karamazov* plumb the darkest depths of the human heart.

LEV (LEO) NIKOLAYEVICH, GRAF TOLSTOY (1828–1910), a Russian count and one of the world's greatest novelists, produced one of the most famous novels ever written – *War and Peace* – and the tragic and unforgettable *Anna Karenina*.

ANTON PAVLOVICH CHEKHOV (1860–1904), a master playwright and short story writer, inspired many imitators with the brooding atmosphere and credible characters of his most famous works – *The Seagull, Uncle Vanya, The Three Sisters* and *The Cherry Orchard*.

Чехова–*muzey Chekhova*), Gorky (Музей Горького–*muzej Gor'kogo*), Dostoevsky (Музей Достоевского–*muzej Dostoevskogo*), Tolstoy (Музей Толстого–*muzej-Tolstogo*) and Mayakovsky (Музей Маяковского–*muzej Mayakovskogo*) museums of literature.

Another world-renowned art collection is housed in the **Tretyakov Art Gallery** (Третьяковская галерея–*Tret'yakovskaya galereya*). The original building and core collection of 1,500 paintings were left to the city of Moscow by the brothers Pavel and Sergey Tretyakov, who, as well as being wealthy 19th-century merchants, were also enthusiastic patrons of the arts. Here you can admire the cream of Russian art, from the early 12th-century Byzantine icon the *Holy Virgin of Vladimir*, to early 20th-century abstract art by Vassily Kandinsky. A collection of 12th- to 17th-century religious art includes several icons painted by the Russian master Andrei Rublev in the 15th century, in particular the famous *Holy Trinity*, which originally graced the Cathedral of the Trinity in Sergiyev Posad (see page 59). Other attractions which may be on view are the disturbing *Ivan the Terrible with the Body of His Son* by Ilya Repin, *Morning of the Execution of the Streltsy* by

Icon in the Tretyakov Art Gallery.

Surikov, *Portrait of Tolstoy* by I.N. Kramskoy and the *Portrait of Dostoevsky* by V.G. Perov.

Around the Garden Ring

Stretching west from Arbatskaya Square, between the Boulevard Ring and Garden Ring, are two streets with the same name, but entirely different characters. **Arbat Street** (улица Арбат—*ulitsa arbat*), a pedestrian precinct lined by buildings which have survived unchanged since the 18th and 19th centuries, is enclosed by a charming district of

Busker on Arbat Street.

narrow, crooked back streets, a reminder of the old Moscow. The Arbat is a prime tourist area, filled with art galleries and souvenir shops, and crammed with buskers, street artists and stalls of *matryoshka* dolls and Russian fur hats. There are pickpockets too, so take care.

In complete contrast, just around the corner, is the **Novy Arbat** (Новый Арбат), a former showpiece of Soviet design. The street, now a busy six-lane highway, was built in the early 1960s under the name Kalininsky Prospekt. Flanked by broad, straight pavements and glass-and-concrete office buildings, apartments and shops, it sliced through part of the old Arbat neighbourhood. It was recently given a face-lift, with grass verges created and trees planted.

Novy Arbat ends just beyond the Garden Ring, at a bend in the Moskva River. Here it is overlooked by the glittering marble walls of the city's **White House,** scene of confrontation between Boris Yeltsin and the hardline communists who tried to overthrow Mikhail Gorbachev in the attempted coup of August 1991. The building houses the administrative offices of the Russian government. Facing it across the river is the Gothic tower of the **Hotel Ukraine** (гостиница Украина– *gostinitsa Ukraina*), one of seven similar buildings – known as Stalin's Seven Sisters – which were erected in Moscow during the late 1940s and early 1950s. The 'Sisters' share the distinguishing features of Gothic ornamentation, huge stepped spires and overpowering size.

At 240 metres (790 feet), the tallest of the seven is the distinctive tower of **Moscow University** (Московский униве-

The Gothic-style tower of the 1950s Hotel Ukraine looks down on busy Kutuzovskij Prospekt.

рситет–*moskovskij universitet*). This is Russia's largest university, hosting 32,000 students from over 100 countries. In front of the university, gardens lead to an observation platform, from where a splendid panoramic view over the city is framed between the charming little Church of the Trinity on the left and the Ski Jump on the right.

In the foreground, prominent on the far bank of the river, spreads **Luzhniki Park** (Лужники), one of Europe's largest sports complexes and the main venue for the 1980 Moscow Olympics. More than 100 million cubic feet of earth was trucked in to raise the 182 hectares (450 acres) of water meadow above flood level. The park has running tracks, tennis courts, a swimming pool, ice rink, sports palace and the huge **Central Lenin Stadium** (Центральный стадион имени Ленина–*tsentral' nyj stadion imeni Lenina*), which has seating for 100,000. International football matches involving Moscow's two main teams, *Spartak* and *Dinamo*, are often played here.

Upstream from Luzhniki, set within a high, crenellated wall, lies the hauntingly beautiful **Novodevichij Convent** (Новодевичий монастырь–*novodevichij monastyr'*), one of the city's

Novodevichij Convent, one of the city's oldest religious centres.

oldest religious centres. The convent was originally a combined military and religious outpost, which grew around the central Cathedral of the Virgin of Smolensk, built in the early 15th century by Grand Prince Vasily III to celebrate his capture of Smolensk from Lithuania. Peter the Great imprisoned his half-sister Sophia here in 1689, accusing her of political intrigue. He even had some of her supporters hanged outside her window, just to show he meant business. In the peace of the **cemetery**, which has a separate entrance, sombre monuments

Monument in the Novodevichij cemetery.

mark the graves of many notable Russian figures. Buried here are writers Anton Chekhov and Nikolay Gogol, composer Sergey Prokofiev, and politicians Anatoly Gromyko and Nikita Khrushchev.

The Garden Ring crosses the Moskva River near **Gorky Park** (Парк культуры и отдыха имени Горького – *park kul'tury i otdykha imeni Gor'kogo*), or, to give it its full title, the 'Central Park of Culture and Leisure named after Maxim Gorky'. This 121-hectare (300-acre) recreation ground offers Moscow's weary city-dwellers grassy lawns, rose gardens and wooded paths, in addition to a boating pond, roller coaster and amusement park. In summer the park is packed with families and couples strolling the leafy avenues, picnicking by the river and watching shows put on by the clowns and jugglers of the Moscow Circus, while in winter the open-air ice rink comes alive with cheery Muscovites thickly swaddled in great coats and furry hats.

The **Central House of Artists** (Центральный дом художника – *tsentral'nyj dom khudozhnika*), across the Garden Ring from the park entrance, is a modern showcase for contemporary Russian arts and crafts. There are also temporary exhibitions here on a diverse range of themes, from Russian religious art to the latest offerings from the West. The rear part of the building is home to the New Tretyakov Gallery, which mounts exhibits of post-1917 Soviet art. The gardens outside the gallery have been used as a last resting place for the cracked and paint-splattered statues of Communist dignitaries, toppled after the demise of the Soviet regime.

OUTLYING ATTRACTIONS

A number of attractions lie several miles outside the city centre, but can be reached by Metro, or by taking an Intourist guided tour. On Kutuzovskiy Prospekt, west of the river, is the distinctive, round **Battle of Borodino Panorama Museum** (музей-панорама Бородинской битвы – *muzej-panorama Borodinskaoj bitvy*). This houses a huge – 115 by 15 metres (350 by 50 feet) – 360° panoramic painting of the Battle of Borodino, which took place 130 km (80 miles) west of Moscow on 26 August 1812. This was an important battle in the 1812 war against Napoleon, and in its aftermath, the Russian leader, Field Marshal Mikhail Kutuzov, decided to abandon Moscow to the enemy *(see page 20)*. A guided tour is highly recommended to get the most out of this vast recreation of the bloody battlefield,

Representation of the Battle of Borodino.

painted in 1912 to mark the centenary of the battle. Just behind the museum, the **Kutuzov Hut** (Кутузовская изба –*Kutuzovskaya izba*) is a reconstruction of the peasant hut where Field Marshal Kutuzov held a council of war with his generals before making the fateful decision to abandon the capital. Nearby, on the main avenue, a triumphal arch celebrates the eventual Russian victory over Napoleon.

One of Moscow's best-known attractions is the All Russia Exhibition Centre (VVTs), but still popularly known by its Soviet-era initials, **VDNKh**, which stands for Exhibit of the Peoples Economic Achievements. The exhibition is a vast propaganda park, originally designed as a showcase for the economic and scientific accomplishments of the Soviet Union, with separate pavilions allotted to each field of endeavour – agriculture, atomic energy, electrification, space, education and engineering, to name but a few. Everything about the exhibi-

A gilded version of Soviet youth at the VVTs exhibition.

tion is grandiose and larger than life, beginning as soon as you exit from the Metro station. Immediately outside is a shimmering titanium obelisk as tall as a 30-storey building, a sweeping, soaring representation of a spacecraft blasting off. The monument and the museum at its base are dedicated to the Russian space programme. From here a wide avenue leads to the enormous triumphal arch at the entrance to the exhibition, topped by the sculpture of two gilded Soviet youths holding aloft a sheaf of wheat. Another oversized monument stands off to the right of the main gate: the 1937 socialist-realist steel sculpture called *Worker and Woman Collective Farmer,* which depicts another two idealised Soviet comrades, holding up a hammer and a sickle. Inside the gates, the pavilions impress thanks to their size and the variety of architectural styles, but alas, not due to their contents. Unfortunately, the ultimate achievement of the Soviet economy was to instigate its own downfall, and many of the pavilions have closed, while others have become shops. Nevertheless, many things are worth seeing, like the magnificent **Gilded fountain** in Friendship of Peoples Square, decorated with golden statues of young women, each dressed to represent one of the original 15 Soviet republics.

Veteran souvenir hunters should take the 20-minute Metro journey to **Izmailovsky Park** (Измайловский парк) for its weekend market. From the Metro exit, turn left and follow the crowds for about 10 minutes to the market entrance. Here you will find hundreds of stalls selling the most amazing variety of goods – carpets, painted wooden eggs, samovars, Palekh boxes, ex-Soviet army caps and jackets, medals, coins, stamps, amber jewellery, fossils and minerals, photographic equipment, flags and banners, model aircraft, busts of Lenin, cigarette cases, hip flasks, old scientific instruments, books, paintings, models of wooden churches made from old lollipop sticks – the list is seemingly endless. Quite apart from potential souvenirs, serious collectors may find objects of interest here, especially relics from World War II. Even if you don't intend on buying anything, the market is a truly fascinating place in which to browse.

On the eastern outskirts of Moscow, the former estate of the wealthy Sheremetev family lies at **Kuskovo** (Куск-)

Kuskovo Palace.

ово). In its heyday this country park was known as the 'Versailles of Moscow', with a late 18th-century stately wooden palace surrounded by 32 hectares (79 acres) of ornamental gardens. The richly decorated palace, which overlooks a lake where Count Sheremetev staged mock sea battles for the amusement of his guests, now houses the Ceramics Museum, with impressive displays of Russian and Oriental china. Look out also for the Grotto and French-style hermitage. Kuskovo is reached either by taking the Metro to Ryazanskiy Prospekt (Рязанский проспект) and then a bus to the estate, or by following a guided tour.

The Church of the Ascension at Kolomenskoe has been faithfully preserved.

Another worthwhile tour run by Intourist is the excursion to the former royal estate of **Kolomenskoe** (Коломенское), which lies about 10 km (6 miles) south of the Kremlin, on a scenic bluff overlooking the river. Independent sightseers should take the Metro to Kolomenskaya (Коломенская) station, from where a 10-minute walk leads to the gate. From the 16th century on a favourite country retreat of Russian rulers, Kolomenskoe has been preserved as an architectural museum.

The magnificent **Church of the Ascension,** built in 1532, forms its centrepiece,

One of the treasures of religious architecture at Kolomenskoe: the heavenly Kazan Church.

representing the first instance when shapes and forms developed in wooden churches were tried in buildings of stone. The graceful 70-metre (230-foot) spire doubled as a look-out tower against Tartars invading from the south. Nearer to the entrance gate is the beautiful 17th-century **Kazan Church**, with its gracefully proportioned sky-blue domes decorated with gold stars.

Part of the estate is used as a museum of wooden architecture, the highlight of which is **Peter the Great's cabin.** This small wooden house was moved here from Arkhangelsk on the northern coast, where Peter stayed for a period in 1702. After viewing the buildings, you can stroll along the paths which wind through the wooded grounds – and which include a number of 600-year-old oak trees – or alternatively, have a picnic by the river and enjoy the Russian countryside.

Day Trips from Moscow

If you can spare only one day for an excursion from Moscow, then the place to head for is undoubtedly **Sergiyev Posad** (Сергиев посад). A 75-km (47-mile) drive northeast of Moscow, this village, which from 1930 to 1991 was known as Zagorsk, is a treasure trove of Russian religious art and architecture. This is where the Trinity Monastery of St Sergiy was founded in 1345 by Sergiy of Radonezh, a monk whose blessing inspired the army of Prince Dmitry of Moscow to triumph over the Tartars in 1380. Sergiy was canonised after his death, and his miraculously preserved remains lie in the **Cathedral of the Trinity**, a small, single-domed church built in 1422, decorated with icons painted by Russian master Andrei Rublev. Rublev's most famous work, the *Holy Trinity*, now hangs in the Tretyakov Art Gallery in Moscow – a copy is in its place in the cathedral's iconostasis. Sergiy was proclaimed as the 'Guardian of Russia', and his posthumous reputation was reinforced when in the 17th century the monastery's defenders successfully held out against a

The Cathedral of the Assumption at Sergiyev Posad.

16-month siege by a 15,000-strong army of invading Poles. Even Peter the Great once took refuge here, when he felt his enemies were closing in.

The monastery's massive walls and towers were built in the mid-16th century, and a decade later the magnificent **Cathedral of the Assumption** was erected in the centre of the precinct, its design inspired by the church of the same name in the Kremlin. Its blue-and-gold, star-studded domes overlook the tomb of Boris Godunov, the only tsar not to be buried either in the Kremlin or in St Petersburg. Try not to miss the monastery **Museum of History and Art,** if it is open; on display is a rich collection of icons, gem-encrusted robes, gold, jewellery and other treasures, as well as exhibits chronicling the history of the monastery.

Timber house at Abramtsevo.

Sergiyev Posad is still a place of pilgrimage for believers from all over Russia, who come to pay their respects to St Sergiy, the most revered saint of their country. The village's other claim to fame is that it is the birthplace of that quintessential Russian souvenir, the *matryoshka* doll. These nesting wooden dolls were first made here at the turn of the 20th century, and are still being produced today.

The estate of **Abramtsevo** (Абрамцево), roughly 60 km (38 miles) to the northeast of Moscow, enjoys several interesting artistic associations. In the mid-19th century, the aristocratic atmosphere of the time was recorded in book form by the owner, Sergei Aksakov, who was also a writer. Among his frequent guests were literary figures like Gogol and Turgenev. Later, the estate was bought by Savva Mamontov, the railway tycoon and art collector, who turned it into an artists' colony dedicated to reviving traditional Russian arts. This lively past is commemorated in a museum in the main house. Abramtsevo can easily be visited on the way to or from Sergiyev Posad.

Less than 26 km (16 miles) west of Moscow city centre, the estate of **Arkhangelskoe** (Архангельское) is a grand reminder of Russia's imperial past. This was once the country estate of Prince Nikolai Yusupov, Director of the Imperial Museums and one of the richest men in all Russia. He used his opulent palace as a showcase for his stunning collection of art, sculpture, china, crystal, tapestry and furniture, and for parties attended by the cream of Russian society. Catherine

Gorki Leninskiye.

the Great was one of his many admirers, and Pushkin was a regular visitor. The palace has now been preserved as a museum, complete with pre-revolutionary decor and furnishings. In the beautiful gardens Yusupov's famous wooden theatre is where the Prince's own company of serf actors regularly trod the boards to amuse his guests. The theatre houses a small museum which chronicles its lively history.

Roughly 30 km (18 miles) southeast of the city centre, the estate of **Gorki Leninskiye** (Горки Ленинские) was a place of great significance to the citizens of the former Soviet Union. Lenin spent his last months in the manor house here (which until 1917 was home to the mayor of Moscow). The great revolutionary, whose firebrand rhetoric inspired the Bolsheviks to seize power in 1917, was crippled in 1922 by a series of strokes which left him unable to speak. He retired to Gorki in May 1923, and died on 21 January 1924. The house is now a museum, preserved as it was in his day, with all the clocks stopped at 6:50 P.M., the moment the Soviet leader drew his final breath.

A very different Russian personality is remembered in the 14th-century town of **Klin** (Клин). This was the home of Pyotr Ilyich Tchaikovsky from 1885 until his death in 1893. His house, now restored, contains many of his possessions, including the Becker grand piano on which he composed both *Sleeping Beauty* and *The Nutcracker,* and his *Fifth* and *Sixth Symphonies.* The piano is played twice a year by leading concert pianists, on the anniversaries of his birth and death (7 May and 6 November). Klin lies 90 km (56 miles) northwest of Moscow, on the main road to St Petersburg.

Intourist also runs day trips to the town of **Gzhel** (Гжель), about 33 km (21 miles) east of Moscow, where the pretty blue-and-white Gzhel china has been made for the last 150 years or so. You can tour the factory and buy the goods at lower prices than you'll find back in the city.

ST PETERSBURG

No visit to Russia is complete until you have seen St Petersburg. Peter the Great's famous city was capital of the Russian empire for 200 years, and gave birth to the October Revolution of 1917. Russia's second-largest city, it is located about 700 km (440 miles) northwest of Moscow, at the head of the Gulf of Finland. It is a major cultural and industrial centre and Russia's principal port.

The city sprawls across the delta of the River Neva, crisscrossed by river channels and canals, a patchwork of islands stitched together by bridges – St Petersburg is often called the 'Venice of the North'. These canals make a **boat trip** a good way to see the sights. Excursions run every day from the beginning of May to the end of October, leaving from jetties beside the Winter Palace and the Admiralty. Smaller boats for exploring the canals can be found at the Anchikov Bridge on Nevskij Prospekt.

The branching river divides the city centre into four sections. Admiralty Side, on the south bank of the Neva, is where much of St Petersburg's cultural heritage is concentrated. Leading out from the Admiralty is Nevskij Prospekt, Russia's most famous thoroughfare, while opposite the Admiralty, in the river's main fork, lies Vasilyevskiy Island. North of the Neva, Petrograd Side is clustered around the Peter and Paul Fortress.

Admiralty Side

Begin your tour in the very heart of St Petersburg, at the palace that was both the seat of Imperial power and the scene of the coup that ended it. The elegant **Palace Square** (Дворцовая площадь – *dvortsovaya ploshchad'*) has been the setting for many dramatic events – Imperial and Soviet mili-

The Admiralty, with its landmark spire.

Palace Square.

tary parades, riots and demonstrations, assassination attempts and the famous storming of the Winter Palace in October 1917. Dominating the square is the 48-metre (155-foot) Alexander Column, a granite monolith which was raised to commemorate Tsar Alexander I's victory over Napoleon in 1812. Although weighing over 700 tons, this single piece of granite is not fastened to the ground – the base is so finely cut that its own weight keeps it upright. The south side of the square is bounded by the magnificent sweep of the General Staff Headquarters. The triumphal arch in the centre is crowned by the Chariot of Victory.

The splendour of the **Winter Palace** (Зимний дворец– *Zimnij dvorets*) lies opposite. Built in the mid-18th century by the young Italian architect Bartolomeo Rastrelli, the Winter Palace was both the seat of the Imperial court and the home of the tsars and tsarinas, from Peter the Great to the ill-fated Nicholas II. The elaborate Baroque façade is painted a striking pastel green, with pilasters, cornices and windows picked out in white and gold; it is topped by rows of statues.

Today the palace is best known as the home of **The Hermitage** (ýрмитаж – *ermitazh*), one of the finest museums of art in the world, on a par with the Louvre in Paris and New York's Metropolitan. The Hermitage contains an amazing 2.7 million items – from prehistoric artefacts to classics of 20th-century art, though about 1.8 million items are from its priceless coin collection. It is said that if you spent only 10 seconds looking at each one, it would take you at least three and a half years to see them all! The collection was started in the 1760s by Catherine the Great and expanded during the succeeding centuries to fill the neighbouring Small Hermitage and Large Hermitage, in addition to the Winter Palace itself.

More important than quantity, however, is the quality of the Hermitage collection – the paintings especially – which cover the history of Western European art (including the biggest collection of French art outside France). It is impossible to do anything more than scratch the surface in a single visit, and a guided tour is recommended.

The splendid Jordan Staircase, glittering with gilt and marble, leads to the first floor, which is where the Western European works are amassed. Highlights of this stunning collection include:

The Jordan Staircase in the Hermitage.

Leonardo da Vinci's 'Benois' *Madonna* and *Madonna Litta*, Titian's *Saint Sebastian* and the sculpture *Crouching Boy* by Michelangelo; 16th- to 18th-century Spanish works, including some by Velázquez, El Greco, Murillo and Goya; works by Dutch and Flemish masters, including Rubens' *Descent from the Cross*, and no fewer than 26 works by Rembrandt, including *Abraham's Sacrifice of Isaac* and *Portrait of an Old Man*;

Lenin and Leningrad

Vladimir Ilyich Lenin (1870–1924) was one of the most important political figures of the 20th century. Founder of the Russian Communist Party, leader of the October Revolution and first head of the Soviet state, Lenin was born Vladimir Ilyich Ulyanov, son of a school inspector in the town of Simbirsk, 643 km (400 miles) east of Moscow. The execution of his elder brother for plotting to assassinate Alexander III impelled the young Ulyanov, who studied law at St Petersburg University, on the road to revolution.

Sentenced to three years in Siberia for subversive activities, he adopted the pseudonym Lenin, and during his subsequent exile in Western Europe he became a leading authority on Marxism. German spies smuggled him back to St Petersburg – or Petrograd as it was then known – in 1917. His leadership gained the support of peasants, soldiers and workers, enabling the Bolshevik Party to seize power in the October Revolution and shape the political future of the Soviet Union.

Following his death in 1924, the Soviet authorities indulged in an orgy of renaming in his honour. Every town and city had its Lenin Square, Street or Avenue, and of course Petrograd, the Cradle of the Revolution, became Lenin City – Leningrad. In June 1991, however, the city voted to restore the original name, St Petersburg.

and the world-famous collection of 19th- and 20th-century French art, including works by Cézanne, Matisse, Monet, Degas, Gauguin, Renoir and Pissarro, and two rooms of early Picasso.

Quite apart from the paintings, the interior of the palace itself is a major attraction. Don't miss: the 1812 Gallery, decorated with over 300 portraits of military leaders who took part in the war against Napoleon, including a large canvas of Field Marshal Kutuzov; the Malachite Hall, with its lavish decoration of bright green stone from the Urals (next door is the White Dining Room, where

The Madonna Litta *by Leonardo da Vinci.*

the Provisional Government was arrested by the Bolsheviks at the time of the storming of the Winter Palace); the sumptuously decorated Gold Drawing Room; and the equally opulent Pavilion Hall, with sparkling chandeliers, a colourful mosaic floor copied from a Roman bath, and little marble fountains that frame the view into Catherine the Great's hanging garden.

Certainly make it a priority to visit the Gold Treasures Gallery and the Jewellery Gallery, both of which feature items from the Scythians and the Ancient Greeks until the 19th century. These rooms contain the most precious gold and jewelled items in the museum – and the entire world. If you only have one day at the museum, you might have to choose between the two. Entrance to each room requires an additional fee, and is possible only by making a reservation several hours before, though it's better to do so a day in advance.

St Petersburg's best-known landmark is the golden spire of the **Admiralty** (Адмиралтейство – *admiraltejstvo*), topped by a weathervane in the shape of a full-rigged ship. The Neo-Classical building occupies the site of Peter the Great's original shipyard, and dates from 1806–1823. The Russian Navy was run from here between 1711 and 1917, and today the Admiralty houses a naval college.

The open space of **Decembrists' Square** (Площадь декабристов – *ploshchad' Dekabristov*), named after the uprising that took place here in December 1825 *(see page 20)*, is at the downstream end of the Admiralty. The focal point of the square is Falconet's striking equestrian statue of Peter the Great – popularly known as the **Bronze Horseman** – which is set above a massive slab of granite. Commissioned by Catherine the Great and unveiled in 1782, it depicts Peter's steed rearing defiantly while tramping underfoot the Snake of Treason.

The Bronze Horseman.

Behind the square rises the vast golden dome of **St Isaac's Cathedral** (Иса-акиевский собор – *isaak-yevskij sobor*), dominating the St Petersburg skyline.

The cathedral, one of the largest in the world, took 40 years (1818–1858) to build, and needed 100 kg (220 lbs) of gold to gilt the dome. The interior, which can hold up to 14,000 worshippers, is lavishly decorated – hardly a square inch of wall or ceiling is left uncovered by murals, mosaics, or gold adornments.

In 1931, the Soviet regime converted the cathedral into an anti-religious museum, explaining the paintings, frescoes and reliefs as 'incidents from

St Isaac's Cathedral.

Christian mythology'. At present, St Isaac's is being renovated, but it remains a museum, though occasionally on high church holidays, such as Easter, services are held here. Climb to the viewing gallery (at the base of the dome), from where there is a panoramic view of St Petersburg at your feet.

Nevskij Prospekt

The street plan of St Petersburg, laid out in the 18th century, has three grand avenues radiating from the focal point of the Admiralty spire. Of the three, **Nevskij Prospekt** (Невский проспект) is generally accepted as the grandest. It is the most famous thoroughfare in Russia, as well as one of the world's great avenues. Extending for 5 km (3 miles) from the Admiralty to the Alexander Nevskiy Monastery, it is thronged with shoppers, office workers, street artists, buskers, students and tourists, and lined with churches, historic buildings, pretty bridges, department stores and restaurants.

Beginning your stroll at the Admiralty end, you will soon reach the grand colonnade of the **Kazan Cathedral** (Казанский собор–*Kazanskij sobor),* inspired by St Peter's in Rome. This sweeping curve of 96 fluted columns has military statues at either end – the one on the left is of Field Marshall Kutuzov – and incorporates a pleasant garden. During the Soviet era, the cathedral building housed a Museum of the History of Religion and Atheism, which was packed with anti-religious propaganda – Karl Marx, the father of Communism, denounced religion as the 'opium of the masses'. The Museum of Religion, as it is now called, is housed in a separate building on Pochstamskaya Street, not far from St Isaac's Cathedral. It is one of the largest collections of religious art and ritual objects in the world.

The Church of the Resurrection of Christ and the Griboyedov Canal.

Here the street crosses the Griboyedov Canal, and there is a fine view along to the multi-coloured domes of the **Church of the Resurrection of Christ** (Храм воскресения Христова – *khram voskreseniya khristova)*, also known as the Church of the Saviour on Spilled Blood *(spasna krovi)*. A St Basil's Cathedral lookalike, it seems a little out of place amid the Baroque and Classical splendour of St Petersburg. A fine example of Classical magnificence is situated between the church and Nevskiy Prospekt in the form of the Square of the Arts (Площадь искусств – *ploshchad' iskusstv)*.

A 12th-century icon in the Russian Museum.

The splendid yellow-and-white building on the north side of the square is the Mikhailovsky Palace (1819–1824), home to the **Russian Museum** (Русский музей – *russkij muzej)*. Its magnificent collection of Russian art ranges from 12th-century religious icons to 20th-century Avant-Garde canvases by the likes of Kandinsky and Malevich, and includes two of Russia's most famous paintings – *Volga Boatmen* and *Zaporozhie Cossacks Writing a Letter to the Turkish Sultan,* both by Ilya Repin (1844–1930). Next door, the Museum of Ethnography is devoted to the folk arts and crafts of the various peoples of the former Soviet Union.

Back on the main street is **Gostinny Dvor** (Гостиный двор–merchants' yard), a two-storeyed warren of tiny shops that serves as a department store. Its crowded arcades and un-smiling staff are best avoided in favour of the open-air **art market** that sets up at the point where the Moika and Gri-boyedov canals meet, in the shadow of the Church of the Res-urrection of Christ. Here you may decide to have your portrait sketched, or to browse among paintings of St Petersburg views, or shop for coffee-table art books which will allow you to take the cream of the Hermitage collection home with you.

Rossi Street (Улица зодчего Росси–*ulitsa zodchego Rossi),* behind the theatre, was named after the architect who designed both the Square of the Arts and the General Staff Headquarters. Carlo Rossi also designed the Pushkin Theatre, as well as laying out this perfectly proportioned street as an approach – it is 22 metres (72 feet) wide and 220 metres (721 feet) long and is flanked by symmetrical façades 22 metres (72 feet) high.

At the beautiful **Anichkov Bridge** (Аничков мост– *Anichkov most),* graced by four bronzes of magnificent rearing horses, Nevskij Prospekt crosses the Fontanka River before continuing a further 2½ km (1½ miles) to the historic **Alexander Nevsky Monastery** (Лавра Алек-сандра Невского–*lavra aleksandra nevskogo),* across the way from the Hotel Moskva. The monastery was found-ed by Peter the Great in 1713, on the site where he believed Prince Alexander of Novgorod (1220–1263) had defeated the Swedish army on the banks of the Neva in 1240, just as Peter himself had done in 1703. After this famous victory he became known as Alexander Nevskiy (Alexander of the Neva), and was then canonised by the Russian Orthodox Church in 1547. The monastery's Cathedral of the Trinity celebrates the Feast of St Alexander Nevisky on 12 September. The main attractions here, however, are the two cemeteries, which contain the graves of many famous Russians, including Mussorgsky, Tchaikovsky, Dostoevsky and Rimsky-Korsakov. The monastery grounds are open to the public, but a guided tour will be necessary for visiting the cemeteries.

Vasilyevskiy Island

One of best views in St Petersburg is enjoyed from the eastern tip of Vasilyevskiy Island, the point known to the locals as the **Strelka** (Стрелка – 'The Spit'). Here you can look across the glittering Neva to the Winter Palace and the Peter and Paul Fortress. The Strelka was once the commercial centre of the port of St Petersburg, and the two **Rostral Columns**, decorated with ships' prows, were used as lighthouses. Stone figures at the base of the columns represent Russia's four mighty rivers that serve as arteries of trade – the Dnieper, Volga, Volkhov and Neva.

A Rostral Column.

Originally the Stock Exchange, the white, Classical building framed between the columns now houses the Naval Museum. Its prime exhibit is the little boat (ботик Петра – *botik Petra*) in which Peter the Great learned to sail and which he later went on to christen the 'Grandfather of the Russian Navy'.

A number of other **museums** clustered on the Strelka include the Zoology Museum, with its famous woolly Siberian mammoth, the Mendeleev Museum (dedicated to the pioneering Russian chemist), the Literature Museum and the Museum of Anthropology and Ethnography. The last is in the distinctive blue-and-white building known as the **Kunstkammer**; among its exhibits you can still gawk at preserved monsters and freaks of nature from Peter the Great's original collection.

Petrograd Side

In May 1703, Peter the Great cut the turf on Hare Island on the north bank of the Neva, starting the first building project of his new city, the **Peter and Paul Fortress** (Петропавловская крепость –*petropavlovskaya krepost'*). The original wood-and-earth defences were replaced with solid stone ramparts, but in 300 years of existence the fort has never been fired upon. By the time it was completed, Peter had vanquished the marauding Swedes, and the city's main defences had been transferred to Kronstadt, an island off the mouth of the River Neva. But the grim fort was put to other uses, notably as Imperial Russia's most notorious political prison.

A number of famous characters who incurred the displeasure of the tsar were

Peter and Paul Fortress with the spire of the Cathedral.

incarcerated in the gloomy cells of the Trubetskoy Bastion, beginning with his own son, Aleksey. Others who followed later included the leaders of the Decembrists, Dostoevsky, Gorky and Trotsky, and Lenin's elder brother Alexander. Listen for the 12 o'clock gun, which is fired from the rampart each day at noon.

In the middle of the fortress rises the graceful spire of the historic **Cathedral of Peter and Paul** (Петропавловский собор–*petropavlovskij sobor),* which was built between 1714 and 1733 by Swiss architect Domenico Trezzini. The slender, golden spire stands 122 metres (400 feet) tall and is topped only by the television tower. The richly decorated interior of the cathedral is the burial place of Peter the Great and most of his successors. His tomb is before the iconostasis, at the far right; locals still come to lay flowers here.

During construction of the fortress, Peter lived in a small wooden cabin a short distance upstream. Built in just three days, **Peter's Cabin** (Домик Петра–*domik Petra)* has been preserved inside a stone building, furnished exactly as it was in his day. Not far beyond the cabin lies the cruiser *Aurora* (Аврора), built in St Petersburg in 1903. This pocket battleship saw action in the Far East during the Russo-Japanese War of 1904–1905, but earned herself a place in the history books in October 1917 when her crew fired a blank shell to signal the start of the Bolshevik assault on the Winter Palace. She was restored and opened as a historic monument in 1956.

Another spot that will forever be associated with the Russian Revolution of 1917 lies across the bridge from the *Aurora,* on the Vyborg Side. When Lenin returned to Petrograd in April 1917 with the help of German spies, he arrived at the **Finland Station** (Финляндский вокзал–*finl'andskij vokzal).* He received a rapturous reception from the local workers and gave a fiery speech from on top of an old

armoured car parked outside the station, an event commemorated in the Lenin statue that is now in the square. To escape the
attention of the authorities, he fled to Finland in August, before
returning in October, when he led the successful Bolshevik
uprising. He travelled incognito on both these journeys, dis-
guised as a stoker on Finland Railways Locomotive number
293. The steam engine was presented by Finland to the
USSR in 1957, and is now displayed inside the station.

Day Trips from St Petersburg

Outside St Petersburg lie the former country estates of the Imperial court. Parks and palaces belonging to Peterhof, Pushkin
and Pavlovsk were all captured and occupied by the Germans
during World War II, and sadly suffered severe damage. Since
then, these magnificent monuments to the power and wealth
of Imperial Russia have been almost completely restored.

Peterhof, the summer residence of Peter the Great.

Top of the list for most visitors is a trip to the summer residence of Peter the Great at **Peterhof** (Петергоф) to see what is probably the finest display of waterworks in the world. The park, set on a bluff overlooking the Gulf of Finland, lies 29 km (18 miles) west of the city. It can be reached by guided tour or suburban train, but the best way to go is by sea; hydrofoils depart regularly from the Neva embankment beside the Winter Palace (summer only). The dazzling opulence of both the palace and gardens was inspired by Versailles, which Peter visited in 1717. The tsar was determined that his own estate should exceed that of the French king in splendour and sophistication.

From the jetty, the tree-lined Water Avenue leads to the **Grand Cascade**, a splendid tribute to the skill and imagination of Peter's engineers. The 64 water jets and 37 golden statues provide a stunning setting for the famous **Samson Fountain**, in which a muscular Samson is shown tearing apart the jaws of a lion. The fountain symbolised Peter's victory over Sweden (whose coat of arms contains a lion), which was achieved on St Samson's Day (27 June) 1709. The water for the cascade, and for the other fountains in the park, is piped from the Ropsha Hills, 22 km (14 miles) to the south. The fountains are turned off from October to April.

At the top of the cascade is the long yellow façade of the **Great Palace**, where the state rooms have had their lavish interiors restored. Photographs show the dreadful condition the palace was left in after the German occupation, and you will marvel at the transformation wrought by the skilled renovation workers. The extensive park also contains a number of other, smaller palaces. **Monplaisir**, down by the sea, was the first to be completed (1714–1722), and became Peter's favourite. Overlooking the sea from his study, he could see across the Gulf of Finland and admire the ships of his newly created navy.

Suburban trains depart regularly from Vitebsk Station (Витебский вокзал–*vitebskiy vokzal*) for the 25-km (16-mile) trip to the village of **Pushkin** (Пушкин), named after the famous poet in 1937 (the centenary of his death), but originally called Tsarskoye Selo (Tsar's Village) because of the parks and palaces that were built there in the 18th century by the empresses Elizabeth and Catherine the Great.

As its centrepiece is the grandiose **Catherine Palace** (Екатерининский дворец–*yekaterininskij dvorets),* a Baroque masterpiece in white, gold and royal blue. It was designed by Bartolomeo Rastrelli (who also designed the Winter Palace), and named after Catherine I (second wife of Peter the Great). The Agate Rooms adjoin the Palace, as do a bath-house decorated with beautifully coloured and polished stone, and the Cameron Gallery, which enjoys a splendid view of the gardens. The palace is also home to the reconstructed Amber Room.

The landscaped grounds are dotted with a variety of pavilions and monuments, many around the fringes of the Great Pond. The lovely Marble Bridge at the far end of the pond leads to the Pyramid, which marks the last resting place of Catherine the Great's favourite pet dogs.

The train to Pushkin continues to **Pavlovsk** (Павловск), a few miles further on. Named after Paul (Pavel in Russian), the son of Catherine the Great, the royal park of Pavlovsk is a masterpiece of landscape architecture. In contrast to the Baroque magnificence of Pushkin, the **Great Palace** is a restrained Classical design in yellow and white, with curving wings enclosing a statue of the Grand Duke Paul. The principal reason for going to Pavlovsk, however, is the 600-hectare (1500-acre) **Park**. Come for a picnic and spend the afternoon exploring the wooded avenues and shady glades, pavilions and ponds.

Both Pushkin and Pavlovsk can be visited by guided tour.

WHAT TO DO

SHOPPING

Shopping in Moscow and St Petersburg is nowhere near as difficult as it has been, even in the recent past, but it is still very different from what most visitors will be used to. The first noticeable difference is that there appears to be no shortage of items to buy, but they are sold in a variety of ways. More formally, there are the old state department stores which are now broken down into small sub-sections; smaller shops specializing in up-market Western brand goods; hotel shops stocking only Western items, many quite luxurious; food shops that are not easy to identify from the outside, in which the supplies seem sparse by Western standards; kiosks which are literally everywhere – these sell a bewildering variety of goods, including soft drinks, beer, cigarettes, spirits, etc.; and now even 24-hour Western-style supermarkets.

Less formally, there is the street selling. This ranges from people who set up a stall, or a box, and sell whatever produce or products they happen to have; lines of people who just seem to appear and disappear outside Metro and train stations who sell loaves, single pieces of fish, bottles of beer and vodka, clothes and whatever else they can find; stalls selling tourist souvenirs; and even people selling their kittens and puppies.

What makes this even more confusing is how you pay. Even though payment with foreign currencies is illegal, the price you are quoted, or that which is on the ticket, is sometimes in US dollars or euros. This price is then multiplied by the current number of roubles to the US dollar/euro; the product is the amount you pay.

*The Gostinny Dvor
department store in
St Petersburg.*

Visitors acclimatised to thinking that there is a shortage of goods, particularly consumer items, will be in for a surprise. It is now possible to buy, openly, every conceivable kind of name-brand goods available elsewhere in the world, as well as day-to-day items such as cigarettes, beer, wines, toiletries, soft drinks, tea, etc.

Remember to take a small pocket calculator with you – it makes it easier when bargaining with people.

Anything that is considered to be of historical or cultural value (in the opinion of the customs officer, that is) cannot be taken out of the country. This includes art, old manuscripts, antiques, coins, medals and so on. Anything bought in a shop or an art gallery is safe enough (keep those receipts!), but you could possibly have trouble with objects bought on the street or in the markets.

Moscow's main shopping areas are in Tverskaya Street, Petrovsky Street and Novy Arbat. The best-known department store is **GUM**, conveniently situated right on Red Square *(see page 39)*. Its main competitor is **TSUM** (ЦУМ), across the street from the Bolshoi Theatre; it gets very crowded here, but can be rewarding for bargain souvenirs such as samovars, fur hats and jewellery. Up the road from TSUM, at 10 Petrovska Street, is **Petrovsky Passage** (Петровский пассаж), a smaller, less crowded, up-market version of GUM.

In St Petersburg, shopping is centred around Nevskiy Prospekt. The two big stores are Gostinny Dvor *(see page 72)* and The Passage.

In both cities, however, it is better to avoid the big shops and head for the **street markets**. In Moscow, most tourists head for the Arbat *(see page 48)*, which is crammed with souvenir stalls, though the weekend market at Izmailovsky Park *(see page 54)* is bigger and more interesting. In St - Petersburg, souvenir hunters should make their way to the market situated near the Cathedral of the Resurrection on the Griboyedov Canal. In all these places it's possible to haggle over prices.

What to Buy

Amber: Russia's Kalingrad region on the Baltic coast produces around 90 percent of the world's amber. This translucent, golden, fossilized pine resin is carved into jewellery – earrings, bracelets and necklaces – as well as figurines.

Art: Paintings can be bought in markets and galleries, and range from views of the Kremlin, through copies of famous pictures, to a lightning quick portrait of yourself.

Books: Even if you can't read Russian, there are many excellent coffee-table books available, including collections of photographs of city sights, architectural studies, or reproductions of the artworks in The Hermitage or Tretyakov.

Caviar and champagne: If you are offered caviar in the street, remember that it is a restricted item, and you must be able to show customs a receipt on departure.

In contrast, Russian champagne is ridiculously cheap and of perfectly acceptable quality provided you specify *sukhoe* (dry).

Cameras: The former Soviet Union was famous for producing sturdy, low-priced photographic equipment. It's still available, but again, receipts are required on departure.

Embroidery: Attractive Ukrainian blouses and lace-work from northern Russia are often available.

Flags and posters: With the fall of the Soviet regime, there is a huge surplus of red flags, Communist party banners, socialist-realist poster art, busts of Lenin, Komsomol (of the Young Communists' League) lapel badges and other Soviet items, which enterprising Russians are capitalising on by selling off to eager tourists.

Fur hats: Traditional Russian winter hats with tie-up ear flaps are always a popular buy. On offer is everything from ex-Soviet military hats to fashion statements in real mink, which are very expensive indeed.

Gzhel pottery: This attractive, blue-and-white china, made in Gzhel, a town near Moscow, is much sought after by Russians and tourists alike.

Lacquered boxes: The finest come from Palekh, a small town where craftsmen painted religious icons until the Revolution, at which time they switched to wooden boxes. The

Fur hats guard against the Russian winter.

designs are original and colourful, and come in many shapes and sizes – cigarette boxes, jewellery boxes, pill boxes – not to mention the bewildering variety of prices. The real thing is expensive, but inexpensive copies are sold in the markets.

Matryoshka dolls: These sets of nesting wooden dolls are the quintessential Russian souvenir. The greater the number of dolls inside, the higher the price – top-quality sets are very expensive. An amusing development is the political *matryoshka*, featuring Russian leaders such as Putin, Gorbachev, Brezhnev,

Matryoshka dolls come in various sizes.

Stalin and Lenin, as well as international newsmakers including George W. Bush and Osama Bin Laden.

Music: For visitors with record collections, Russian vinyl is a real bargain, especially for classical music. Cheap CDs and DVDs are available at Moscow's Gorbusha market.

Rugs and carpets: Centuries-old designs from the Central Asian republics of the former USSR still find their way to Moscow. Beware of the problems of shipping purchases home, however, and of the restrictions on exporting articles of cultural or artistic value. It's safest to stick to official shops.

Samovars: Colourfully decorated, charcoal-burning water boilers for traditional Russian tea-making.

Stamps: Serious philatelists can hunt down some interesting oddities among the stalls at Izmailovsky Park *(see page 54)*.

T-shirts: Stalls in the Arbat are piled high with T-shirts adorned with colourful, witty slogans, from plain *perestroika* and *glasnost* to clever send-ups of Western designs.

Vodka: The safest place to buy a bottle of the national nip is at the airport duty-free shops, which offer good values. If you buy from a street kiosk you can't be sure what you'll get. Locals disagree as to whether *Stolichnaya* (Столичная – Capital City) or *Moskovskaya* (Московская– Moscow) is the better tipple, although both are good value. Russky Standard is also a fine brand.

Flavoured varieties include pepper vodka (Перцовка – *pertsovka*) and lemon vodka (Лимонная – *limonnaya*).

Watches: No one can escape Moscow without being offered a 'genuine Soviet Army watch as worn by cosmonauts.' Russian watches can certainly be attractive and reliable, but remember that there's no guarantee attached.

Wooden carvings: Carved spoons, cups and bowls from the village of Khokhloma, brightly painted in traditional red-and-gold designs, are cheap and attractive.

The main shops are usually open from 8 or 9am to 9pm. Monday to Saturday, with an hour's break for lunch.

ENTERTAINMENT

Ballet, Opera and Concerts

Moscow and St Petersburg are sheer heaven for the culture vulture. Dozens of splendid theatres and concert halls provide a top quality programme catering to all musical tastes: ballet, opera, classical music, choral recitals and drama.

A weekly list of attractions is posted at hotel service desks, where you will usually be able to obtain tickets at short notice.

The lavish interior of the Yusupov Theatre in St Petersburg.

If the **Bolshoi Theatre** is sold out, have a look at what's on at the **Stanislavsky Nemirovich-Danchenko Musical Theatre**, where the quality of performance is just as high. Fortunately the Bolshoi Theatre occasionally forsakes its lavish 2,150-seat home for the 6,000-seat **Palace of Congresses** in the Kremlin – a move which significantly increases the odds of managing to secure a ticket.

If you would prefer to attend a concert, it's worth considering either the excellent **State Symphony Orchestra** or **Moscow Philharmonic**, both of which give regular performances at the Tchaikovsky Concert Hall on Mayakovsky Square, or else visit the Moscow Conservatory, located in Gertsena Street.

St Petersburg boasts the renowned **Mariinsky Ballet and Opera Theatre** (formerly the Kirov), which is of course known as one of the leading ballet companies throughout the world. Famous graduates include Anna Pavlova, Vaslav Nijinskiy, Galina Ulanova, Rudolf Nureyev and Mikhail Baryshnikov. Built in the mid-19th century, the 1,800-seat theatre competes in splendour with Moscow's Bolshoi. Many of Russia's most well-known ballets and operas – including Mussorgsky's *Boris Godunov*, as well as Tchaikovsky's *Sleeping Beauty* and *The Nutcracker* – were first performed on this stage. The city's second ballet and

Russian Composers

Russia's greatest 19th-century composers all began their careers in uniform, either as civil servants or junior officers in the military.

MIKHAIL IVANOVICH GLINKA (1804–1857), who endured four stultifying years as a clerk in the Ministry of Communications, was the first Russian composer to have his music played in the West. Extracts from his operas *A Life for the Tsar* (also called *Ivan Susanin*) and *Ruslan and Lyudmila* were performed in Paris in 1845.

Modest PETROVICH MUSSORGSKY (1839–1881), briefly an officer of the guard in St Petersburg and for many years a civil servant (also in the Ministry of Communications), composed Russia's great nationalist opera *Boris Godunov* and the melancholy piano suite *Pictures from an Exhibition*.

PETER ILYICH TCHAIKOVSKY (1840–1893) was employed as a senior clerk in the Justice Ministry before writing 11 operas, six symphonies, the 1812 *Overture* and the three immortal ballets *Swan Lake, Sleeping Beauty and The Nutcracker*.

NIKOLAI ANDREYEVICH RIMSKY-KORSAKOV (1844–1908) composed his first symphony on board ship while a naval cadet. Later he was employed as an inspector of military bands and wrote the evocative symphonic poems *Scheherazade* and *Capriccio Espagnol*.

opera venue is the **Maly Theatre**, which is on the Square of the Arts, and there are several small theatres such as the Yusupov Theatre in the Yusupov Palace.

Performances of **classical music** can be enjoyed at several concert halls. These varied venues include, in St Petersburg, the Maly Philharmonic Hall, the Bolshoi (Shostakovich) Philharmonic Hall and the Glinka Kapella (choral hall), among others.

Performances in St Petersburg.

Festivals

There are three main arts festivals held each year.

The **Golden Mask Festival** (early April), when the best Russian dance, opera, music and theatre companies converge on the capital.

The **St Petersburg White Nights Festival of the Arts** (around the summer solstice, approximately 1 June–1 July), held during midsummer nights when the sun hardly sets. Performances of music, opera, ballet and theatre take place in the city. There is also general merrymaking in the streets, bars and restaurants.

The **Winter Arts Festival** (25 December–5 January) in St Petersburg is one of the city's premier cultural events in winter, featuring many international ballet and classical music stars.

The Circus

Of universal appeal and as popular with Russians as with foreign tourists, the world-famous **Moscow Circus** plays to packed houses six nights a week. Adults and children alike will enjoy the colourful spectacle of acrobats, trapeze artists, horseback riders, jugglers and performing animals. The clowns will raise a laugh even if you don't understand a word of Russian – a pie in the face is a pie in the face in any language.

Moscow has two circuses: one on Tsvetny Boulevard, and called the Old Circus; and the other near Moscow University, across the street from Universitet Metro station.

St Petersburg also has its own circus, which can be found a few blocks north of Anichkov Bridge, on the Fontanka.

Nightlife

Back in the bad old days of Soviet rule, describing Russian nightlife was easy – there wasn't any. But with the rise of the new enterprise culture, the night scene in Moscow, and especially in St Petersburg, is looking up. A new wave of joint venture nightspots has appeared, covering every preference,

Jazz in St Petersburg

Strange though it may seem, St Petersburg has produced some excellent jazz musicians, and the city has three jazz clubs where local bands jam well into the small hours of the morning – the Jazz Philharmonic Hall on Zagorodniy Prospekt, the Neo Jazz Club on Solyanoi Pereulok and the JFC Jazz Club on Shpalernaya Street.

You can also tap your feet to jazz in the street, with bands busking in St Petersburg on Nevskij Prospekt, outside the Winter Palace and near the cruiser *Aurora*.

from an Irish pub serving draught Guinness to a sophisticated casino in Moscow's Savoy Hotel. There are bars, nightclubs and discos of varying quality. When you're planning a night out, we recommend that you check the local press for the latest hot spots *(see page 117)*.

Then again, you can do as the locals do and have a night out in a traditional Russian restaurant. A night out means just that – the food is a secondary consideration and you can reasonably expect to spend all evening drinking vodka and Russian champagne, talking, laughing, singing, dancing, and if you are lucky, occasionally eating. These restaurants – ask your hotel to recommend one – have a dance floor and a cabaret-style show that gets more and more risqué as the evening goes on.

SPORTS

The big spectator sports in Moscow and St Petersburg are **soccer** and **ice hockey.**

Moscow's three top-class soccer teams – *Dinamo, Torpedo and Spartak* – often take part in European competitions. International matches are held at the Central Lenin Stadium in Luzhniki Park *(see page 50)*. The Dinamo Stadium is near the Dinamo Metro station, on Leningradskiy Prospekt. Ice-hockey matches are played in the Sports Palace or at the Luzhniki Small Sports Arena.

The St Petersburg football team, *Zenit*, has also recently emerged as a top national contender. Matches are played at the Kirov Stadium in the far northwest corner of the city.

If you enjoy the occasional flutter, you can wager holiday money at Moscow's 150-year-old Hippodrome, where both **horse-racing** and **trotting** are on the card on Wednesday and Friday evenings and Sunday afternoons. Hard going is not usually a problem, since in winter the horses in fact wear spiked shoes.

EATING OUT

The standard of dining in Moscow and St Petersburg has improved tremendously in recent years, and some of the world's top chefs are now eager to work in these cities. In both places, wonderful meals can be had at budget and high-end prices, and you may also be impressed by the new Russian flare for both exquisite and quirky interior design.

WHERE TO EAT

In Russia the word *restoran* (ресторан) has a more specific meaning than in the West. It refers not only to a place to eat out, but also a place to be entertained. It's an establishment catering mainly to parties and large groups who are out for the whole evening, with live music, dancing and a glitzy floor show. They are not keen on single diners – you'd probably have to share a table. Service is slow, the atmosphere loud and smoky and the food merely adequate. (It is ironic that 'bistro', which is generally a fast service restaurant, is derived from the Russian word быстро which means 'quickly', because the concept hasn't really taken off here yet.) Reservations are necessary and usually have to be made before lunchtime on the same day (your hotel reception desk will do this for you). Eating times at a Russian *restoran* are generally 2–3pm for lunch and 7–9pm for dinner.

In the past several years, Moscow and St Petersburg have developed their own Russian fast food chains, as a kind of answer to McDonald's. The latter is very popular and can be found all over both cities. Budget bistros, where one can get a full meal for about US$6, are now very popular, especially during lunchtime.

At the high end, both cities offer fine restaurants to rival anything in the west in terms of interior and cuisine.

Service at these places is usually very good, and staff speak English. Most establishments now accept credit cards, but it's always wise to have enough cash on hand because credit card machines sometimes break.

WHAT TO EAT

Breakfast (завтрак–*zavtrak*)

Visitors on group tours will usually have all their meals arranged, while independent travellers will probably have breakfast included in the price of their room. Breakfast is a filling affair, consisting of a spread of bread, butter, jam, yoghurt, cheese, eggs, salami, smoked fish, sausages, potato cakes and *blini* stuffed with meat, washed down with grape juice, tea (without milk), or coffee. *Kasha* (porridge) is a traditional breakfast dish and is made of milk and oats, buckwheat or semolina.

Lunch (обед–*obed*)

Enjoying a good lunch requires a bit of planning, especially in Moscow, as distances are great and you can't expect a decent restaurant on every corner. Pick an establishment near where you will be in the morning, and then get there early so that you don't have

Ordering a coffee in Moscow.

to queue for a table. Alternatively – and often more easily – make do with a snack or sandwich from a café or pavement kiosk, and then fill up in the evening.

Dinner (ужин–*uzhin*)

Dinner is usually served between 6 and 10pm. Both cities offer a wide variety of ethnic and international cuisines. Japanese food has recently become very popular in Russia, though it's still hard to find a good Italian restaurant. Of course, it might be better to stick with the local ethnic cuisines – Russian, Georgian, Uzbek, etc.

Popular Dishes

Russian cuisine is generally country fare, with hearty dishes based on meat, fish, cabbage and potatoes, spiced up by regional variations from the surrounding republics. Some dishes have existed for centuries; some have been added from outside influences and have been incorporated into the national menu. Georgian cuisine is particularly diverse and delicious with many Middle-Eastern influences.

Appetisers (закуски–*zakuski*)

A traditional Russian dinner begins with a range of starters, which is almost a meal in itself.

Blini (блины): Small pancakes that are wrapped around a filling such as caviar, sour cream, smoked salmon, honey, or jam.

Caviar (икра–*ikra*): Salty fish roe – black caviar from sturgeon, red from salmon – is usually served with buttered toast or *blini*, sour cream and a slice of lemon. It is both an acquired and alarmingly expensive taste.

Fish (рыба–*ryba*): Bite-sized pieces of smoked salmon or pike-perch, salted sprats, pickled herring and sturgeon in aspic all go well with a shot of vodka, and are very popular.

Salad (салат–*salat*): The most popular salad is a mixture of cucumber, carrot, diced potato, hard-boiled egg, ham and onion, all of which is folded into a rich mayonnaise dressing. This is often known as *salat stolichniy*, or 'Capital City' salad.

Other salads are coleslaw, or simply tomato-and-cucumber. Amongst other favourite *zakuski* are dishes of thinly-sliced and casseroled chicken or beef (жульен–*zhulyen*) and salami (колбаса–*kolbasa*) with bread and mushrooms baked in sour cream (грибы в сметане–*gribi v smetane*).

Soups (суп–*sup*)

Borscht (борЦ–*borshch*): This soup, known all over the world, is actually Ukranian – a hot and hearty red broth of beetroot, cabbage and chunks of boiled beef, garnished with a dollop of sour cream – ideal for those cold Russian winters.

Bulyon (бульон): A simple chicken broth accompanied by noodles or croutons. A popular variation is steamed dumplings stuffed with chopped meat,

Café La Paris in St Petersburg.

known as *pel'meni* (пельмени). The dumplings may also appear as a starter or main course, seasoned with a dash of vinegar or a little sour cream.

Okroshka (окрошка): Something of an acquired taste, this summer soup is served chilled and contains cucumber, onion, hard-boiled egg, thin slivers of meat and the secret ingredient, *kvass*, a beer-like beverage made from fermented rye bread. Try it at least once.

Shchi (Щи): One of Russia's least imaginative dishes, this basic peasant soup consists of either sauerkraut or cabbage.

Solyanka (солянка): A popular soup made from cucumber and tomato, which are mixed with chunks of fish or meat and garnished with chopped olives and a twist of lemon.

Main Courses (Горячие блюда–*goryachie blyuda*)

Beef Stroganoff (беф-строганов–*bef-stroganov*): A traditional and classic main course, named after the *Stroganovs* (Строгановы) merchant family that controlled Siberia in the time of Ivan the Terrible. It consists of thin strips of beef tenderloin braised in a sauce made with wild mushrooms, onions and sour cream.

Chicken Kiev (котлеты по-киевски–*kotlety po-kievski*): Although this rich concoction might not be Russian – it is, in fact, a Ukrainian dish – it has become a recognisable standard feature on international menus all over the world. Tender chicken fillets stuffed with melted butter are sizzled to a mouth-watering golden brown. (Go easy with the knife and fork to avoid a splattering.)

Chicken Tabaka (цыплята табака–*tsyplyata tabaka*): A classic Georgian dish, in which chicken is flattened, spiced, seasoned and marinated, and then fried on a buttered skillet before being served with chopped onion and a portion of hot garlic sauce on the side. Salted and peppery, and a Muscovite favourite.

Fish dishes (рыбные блюда – *rybnye blyuda*): Fish dishes are usually based on sturgeon, salmon, or pike-perch, from the freshwater lakes and rivers of the interior. On the whole their treatment tends not to be very adventurous, the choice being either baked or steamed in a white sauce, or fried and served with tartar sauce.

Pilaf (плов – *plov*): This dish of rice, which is prepared with pieces of lamb or chicken and a mixture of vegetables, can stand either as a meal in itself or provide an accompaniment to a main course.

Shashlik (шашлык): Kebabs – skewered chunks of mutton, onion, mushroom and capsicum – grilled over a charcoal fire and served with a spicy tomato sauce. A very popular dish in Moscow.

Steak (бифштекс – *bifshteks*): This can be something of a gamble. Locally produced Russian beef is not always very good, but you should hopefully get a nice juicy piece of imported beef.

Desserts (сладкие блюда – *sladkiye blyuda*)

Blini (блины): Tasty pancakes which make as good a dessert as an appetizer *(see page 92)*, but with a sweet filling instead of savoury. Try lemon juice, jam, cream, or honey, then sprinkle the lot with icing sugar.

Ice cream (мороженое – *morozhenoe*): This appears to be the favourite food in Moscow and St Petersburg. Vendors sell it on the street in both summer and winter, even if the weather is so cold that a freezer isn't needed to prevent the tempting sweet from melting. Ice cream is also the dessert most often ordered in restaurants, and it comes in

Classic Russian fare – black caviar, washed down with a glass of chilled vodka.

all manner of splits, sundaes and other concoctions, as well as a wide range of flavours.

Pastries (пирожное–*pirozhnoe*): These range from plain biscuits to tiny meringues and pies filled with jam, through to more exotic fare such as rum baba (ромовая баба–*romovaya baba*).

Siberian omelette (сибирский омлет–*sibirskij omlet*), or 'surprise omlette' (омлет сюрприз–*omlet syurpriz*), is better known by most as good old Baked Alaska – ice-cream cooked in the oven.

Drinks (напитки–*napitki*)

Vodka (водка): The national drink is distilled from fermented wheat or rye, and has been produced in Russia ever since the 14th century. The name means 'little water', and it is traditionally drunk neat and chilled, ideally straight from the freezer.

After toasting the assembled company, your glass is then downed in one shot. Refusal to participate is considered an affront, and the idea of mixing this water of life with anything else – including orange juice or tonic water – is tantamount to treason.

Like almost everything in Russia, vodka is valued and sold by weight. The normal measure – 100 grams – is approximately a double.

Brandy (коньяк–*Konyak*): To the eternal disgust of French producers, the Russians persist in calling this 'cognac'. It comes from the wine-growing regions of Georgia and Armenia, is often excellent, and is sometimes drunk at the beginning of the meal instead of at the end.

Wine (вино–*vino*): Hailing from the vineyards of Georgia, the Crimea, Hungary and Bulgaria, wine is widely available in Moscow and St Petersburg restaurants. A couple of recommended wines are *Mukuzani*, a full-bodied red, and *Tsinandali*, a refreshing dry white.

Beer (пиво–*pivo*): Russian beer has come a long way since Soviet times, and is now even exported to the West. St Petersburg is the capital of Russian beer.

Mineral water (минеральная вода–*mineralnaya voda*): Because the tap water is not safe to drink, mineral water is now very popular. Russian brands such as *Borzhom* (боржом), however, have a strong and unpleasant taste, while *Kompot* (компот) – water flavoured with fruit – is sometimes offered in cheaper restaurants.

To Help You Order...

| Waiter | официант | *ofitsiant* |
| Waitress | официантка | *ofitsiantka* |

Could we have a table?	Пожалуйста столик?	*pozhaluysta stolik*
Do you have a set menu?	Есть ли у вас комплексный обед?	*yest' li u vas kompleksniy obed*
I'd like a/ an/some …	Принесите пожалуйста …	*prinesite pozhaluysta*
appetisers	закуски	*zakuski*
beer	пиво	*piva*
bread	хлеба	*khleba*
breakfast	завтрак	*zavtrak*
coffee	кофе	*kofye*
desserts	сладкие блюда	*sladkiye blyuda*
dinner	ужин	*uzchin*
fish	рыбу	*ribu*
fruit	фрукты	*frukty*
glass	стакан	*stakan*
lunch	обед	*obed*
main course	горячие блюда	*goriachie blyuda*
meat	мясо	*myaso*
menu	меню	*myenyo*
milk	молока	*moloka*
mineral water	минеральной воды	*minyeral'noy vodi*
napkin	салфетку	*salfyetku*
salad	салат	*salat*
sandwich	бутерброд	*butyerbrod*
soup	суп	*sup*
sugar	сахар	*sakhar*
tea	чай	*chay*
wine	вино	*vino*

… and Read the Menu

апельсины	*apyel'sini*	oranges
бифштекс	*bifshteks*	beefsteak
битки	*bitki*	meatballs
блины	*blini*	pancakes
говядина	*govyadina*	beef
ветчина	*vetchina*	ham
грибы	*gribi*	mushrooms
икра	*ikra*	caviar
картофель	*kartofyel'*	potatoes
капуста	*kapusta*	cabbage
колбаса	*kolbasa*	cold cuts
курица	*kuritsa*	chicken
лимон	*limon*	lemon
морковь	*morkov'*	carrots
мороженое	*morozhenoye*	ice-cream
осётр	*osyotr*	sturgeon
огурец	*ogurets*	cucumber
персики	*persiki*	peaches
пирожные	*pirozhniye*	pastries
помидоры	*pomidori*	tomatoes
рис	*ris*	rice
ростбиф	*rostbif*	roast beef
салат	*salat*	salad
свинина	*svinina*	pork
сельдь	*syel'd'*	herring
сёмга	*syomga*	salmon
сыр	*sir*	cheese
сосиски	*sosiski*	sausage
судак	*sudak*	pike-perch
цыплёнок	*tsiplyonok*	chicken
шашлык	*shashlik*	shashlik (kebab)
яйца	*yaytsa*	eggs

HANDY TRAVEL TIPS

An A–Z Summary of Practical Information

A

ACCOMMODATION (гостиница – *gostinitsa*)
(See also CAMPING, YOUTH HOSTELS and the list of RECOMMENDED
HOTELS starting on page 129)

In the former Soviet Union, all tourist hotels were run by Intourist, a
state-controlled organisation. Since the liberalisation of trade, many
Western hotel management companies have set up partnerships with
the revamped Intourist and other Russian operators. These joint ventures (JVs) are renovating ageing hotels, retraining staff and generally
raising hotel standards to levels comparable with those in the West.
However, with the ever-increasing stream of tourists, supply is having
difficulty keeping up with demand, particularly in St Petersburg
where new legislation has been pushed through supporting the construction of new hotels. On the whole, the situation in both Moscow
and St Petersburg is improving, but you may well find that hotels are
expensive for what you get. Luckily, there are alternatives for the
budget traveller; in this regard, the recently established Russian Youth
Hostel Association (see HOSTELS) – with hostels in both cities – is an
important addition to the hotel scene. If you are taking a package tour
(still one of the cheapest ways to visit Russia), it is unlikely that you
will be offered a choice of hotels. Any hotels can be dealt with direct-
ly, or through a travel agent. Whichever way you travel, all your
accommodation must be booked in advance, as you will need to show
confirmed hotel reservations when applying for a visa (see CUSTOMS
AND ENTRY FORMALITIES). This is all taken care of if you arrange your
accommodation and visa through your travel agent. Arrangements
should be made as far in advance as possible; a minimum of four to
six weeks is recommended.

You must hand over your passport for registration when you check
in at your hotel, but don't forget to pick it up the next day. All hotels
have a service desk with English-speaking staff who can organise
guided tours, obtain tickets for the opera and ballet, make travel
arrangements and give general assistance.

Moscow & St Petersburg

A popular way of visiting Russia is by staying with a host family. Families are carefully vetted and selected mostly from the staff of local universities; at least one member of each family speaks English. The scheme has proved extremely successful. Full details and the necessary visa invitation are available from HOFA (Host Families Association), which can be contacted through the website <www.hofa.ru> or tel./fax: (812) 275 1992 or (812) 275 5465 or (911) 914 2762 (mobile).

a double/single room	**номер на двоих/ на одного**	*nomer na dvoikh/na odnovo*
with bath/without bath	**с ванной/без ванны**	*s vannoy/bez vanny*
What's the rate per night?	**Какая плата за сутки?**	*kakaya plata za sutki*

AIRPORTS (аэропорт – *aeroport*)

Moscow's international airport, Sheremetyevo II (Шереметьево), is 32 km (20 miles) northwest of the city centre. Facilities include a restaurant, news-agent, souvenir shop, duty-free shop, currency exchange office, post office, left luggage, nursery and car rental desk. Other options are taxi or the airport bus. Bus number 517 goes to Planermaya metro station, and 551 to Rechnoy Vokzal metro; from here take the metro to the city centre. Internal flights from Moscow to St Petersburg leave several times a day from Sheremetyevo I, which is a 20-minute bus ride from Sheremetyevo II. Facilities at Terminal I are very basic – post office, poorly-stocked tea counter, a few kiosks – while it awaits expansion and modernisation.

St Petersburg's international airport is Pulkovo II, which is 17 km (11 miles) south of the city centre, complete with a new terminal building. Domestic flights, including the Moscow shuttle, arrive at Pulkovo I, a 10-minute bus ride from Terminal II. A taxi from the airport to the city centre takes around 30 minutes. An airport express bus service runs between Pulkovo I and the downtown terminal at Ulitsa Bolshaya Morskaya 13, near the Astoria Hotel. There is a bus and a cheap private minibus service between Pulkovo II and the city air terminal on Moskovskiy Prospekt, near the Pulkovskaya Hotel.

B

BUDGETING for YOUR TRIP

Most travellers will have paid for all their accommodation, travel and perhaps meals, too, before leaving home. To give you some idea of what to expect, here are some average prices in US dollars. These can only be regarded as approximate, however, since inflation continues to push costs up.

Airport transfer. Taxi from Sheremetyevo II to Moscow city centre, $50. Taxi from St Petersburg centre to Pulkovo II, $30.

Camping. At Retur Motel-Camping, near St Petersburg, $12 a night.

Car rental. With driver, $10–20 an hour; without driver, approximately $30–50 a day.

Entertainment. A box at the Bolshoi or Mariinsky (Kirov) Theatre, $40–50; Moscow Circus, $13.

Hotels. (Double room with bath, including breakfast). Deluxe from $300 upward, middle range $120–200, budget $30–120.

Meals and drinks. In moderate restaurants catering to tourists, expect $20–60 a head. Cup of coffee, $1–3. Glass of imported beer, $3.

Sightseeing. Museums and art galleries usually have a sensible two-tier pricing policy; one for Russians, which is very low, and one for foreigners, which is closer to Western prices. To see everything in the Kremlin will cost around US$30 and entrance to the Hermitage is about US$10. In addition, if you want to use a camera or camcorder in the latter, there are extra charges.

Taxis. Take great care, as rates vary greatly and **must** be agreed before commencing the journey. Taxis that run on the meter do tend to cheat.

CAMPING (кемпинг–*kemping*)

Russian campsite accommodation is very limited. The choice is either a two or three-berth chalet, or a site for a tent or caravan with use of electricity, showers, toilets, and cooking and laundry facilities. Moscow's Butovo campsite lies 24 km (15 miles) south of the city (tel. 095-548 7900). In St Petersburg, the Olgino campsite, on the Gulf of Finland 17 km (11 miles) west of the city, operates from mid-May through October (tel. 812-238 3550). A safer, more comfortable option is Retur Motel-Camping, 29 km (19 miles) south of the city on the Gulf of Finland, accessible by bus and open all year round (tel. 812-437 7533; <www.retur.ru>).

CAR RENTAL (прокат автомобиля–*prokat avtomobilya*)

A rental car, with or without driver, can be arranged in advance by a travel agent, or through your hotel. Alternatively, you can rent from one of the new rental agencies that are now opening. Cars are rented by the hour, day, or week; you will need an international driving licence, and must be over 21 years of age. Check the car thoroughly before leaving to make sure that everything is in working order, and that any dents or scratches have been recorded on the rental agreement. As roads and driving conditions in the cities are poor, you are recommended to hire a car with driver.

Europcar: Hotel Mezhdunarodnaya, Moscow; tel. (095) 253 1369.

Hertz: Leninskij Prospekt 152, Moscow; tel. (095) 578 5676; Malaya Morskaya Ulitsa 23, St Petersburg; tel. (812) 324 3242; <www.hertz.spb.ru>.

CLIMATE and CLOTHING

Moscow's climate can be extreme, and ranges from around -22°F (-30°C) in the depths of an average winter to 86°F (30°C) during summer heat waves. St Petersburg, though further north, has a climate moderated by the sea, with slightly milder winters and cooler summers. Summer lasts roughly from May to early September, and is usually comfortably warm in both cities, with daytime temperatures between 65°F (18°C) and 75°F (24°C).

St Petersburg is famous for its 'White Nights', from mid-June to early July, when darkness lasts only two hours. Winters are long, cold and dark, with the first snows falling any time between October and December. St Petersburg pays for its white nights in midwinter, when it receives only 5 hours of gloomy daylight. The spring thaw sets in around March or April.

Moscow		J	F	M	A	M	J	J	A	S	O	N	D
average daily	°F	3	8	18	34	46	51	55	53	45	37	26	15
min.	°C	-16	-14	-8	1	8	11	13	12	7	3	-3	10
average daily	°F	15	22	32	50	66	70	73	72	61	48	35	24
max.	°C	-9	-6	0	10	19	21	23	22	16	9	2	-5

St Petersburg													
average daily	°F	8	11	18	33	42	51	55	55	47	39	28	18
min.	°C	-13	-12	-8	0	6	11	13	13	9	4	-2	-8
average daily	°F	19	22	32	46	59	68	70	69	60	48	35	26
max.	°C	-7	-5	0	8	15	20	21	20	15	9	2	-3

Clothing. In summer, light cotton clothes, a sweater and a raincoat are all you need. Formal dress is rarely necessary, even for a night at the opera, though of course you can dress up if you wish. Shorts are frowned upon anywhere other than at the beach.

During winter you will need a warm coat, gloves, a hat or scarf that keeps your ears warm, and waterproof footwear with cleated soles to grip on snow, ice and slush. Buildings are kept very warm indoors in winter, and it is normal to have your coat and hat checked when visiting museums, theatres and restaurants.

COMPLAINTS (жалобы – *zhaloby*)

Complaints should be taken up with the management of the hotel, restaurant, or shop involved.

Before complaining too loudly, however, remember that Russia is going through difficult times. It will be a few years before the standards of service that, for example, visitors from the UK and US take for granted penetrate all corners of Russian life.

CRIME (преступность–*prestupnost*)

You should take the usual precautions against theft – leave your valuables in the hotel safe, not in your room; don't carry large amounts of cash; and beware of pickpockets in crowded areas. Never leave your bags or valuables on view in a parked car – take them with you or lock them in the boot (trunk).

Any theft or loss must be reported immediately to the police in order to comply with your travel insurance. If your passport is lost or stolen, you should also inform your consulate. Unfortunately, crime is on the increase in Russia. Tourists should be particularly aware of gangs of gypsy children who wait around Red Square and the Arbat, harassing visitors by grabbing coats and bags – keep all valuables secure in inside pockets or use a money belt. Stay clear of Gorky Park at night, and watch out for illegal money-changers and for prostitutes.

Luggage theft at Sheremetyevo Airport is also a problem. If at all possible, take carry-on luggage only with you. If this is not an option, try not to travel with expensive-looking suitcases and avoid putting your valuables in checked luggage.

I want to report a theft. **Меня обокрали.** *menya obokrali*

CUSTOMS (таможенный контроль–*tamozhennyj kontrol*)
and ENTRY FORMALITIES

Visitors to Russia need a visa and full passport (a British Visitor's passport is not acceptable) valid for at least three months after your return. Visa applications require photocopies of the front pages of the old-style British passport and back pages of the new-style European passport, three passport photographs, written confirmation of your accommodation arrangements for each night of your stay, and a handling fee.

The easiest way to cope with all this is to have a travel agent deal with both accommodation and visa application. Allow plenty of time – four to six weeks minimum is recommended. Your visa, which is a separate piece of paper – nothing is stamped in your passport – will indicate how long you may remain in Russia, and which cities you may visit.

When your visa is issued, you will also be sent a customs declaration form on which to declare all money and valuables that you intend bringing into the country. Once in Russia, your hotel will take your passport and visa to register you with the local authorities. It is not necessary to enter on the customs declaration every transaction you make. However, you cannot take out more money, in any currency, than you took in. Therefore, if you haven't entered the original transaction and you are left with many roubles, the figures on both customs forms will not tally, and this could cause problems. It is also possible, when changing back roubles, to take different currencies and only enter on the customs forms the amounts you want.

A second customs declaration must be completed at the end of your trip, showing how much currency you are taking out. Both forms must be surrendered on departure. Look after your visa and customs form – lost documents are awkward and time-consuming to replace, and could delay your departure. If you do lose them, contact your hotel service desk. Keep a separate note of your visa number.

Currency restrictions. At present there is no limit to the amount of foreign currency you can take into Russia; importing and exporting Russian notes and coins is prohibited.

The table below shows what you may take into Russia and, when returning, into your own country.

Into:	Cigarettes		Cigars		Tobacco	Spirits		Wine
Russia	1,000		1,000	or	1,000g	1.5l	or	2l
Australia	200	or	250	or	250g	1l	or	1l
Canada	200	or	50	or	900g	1.14l	or	1.14l
Ireland	200	and	50	or	250g	1l	and	2l
N. Zealand	200	or	50	or	250g	1l	and	4.5l
S. Africa	400	and	50	and	250g	1l	and	2l
UK	200	or	50	or	250g	1l	and	2l
US	200	and	100	and	*	1l	and	2l

*a reasonable quantity

D

DRIVING in MOSCOW and ST PETERSBURG

A car is not necessary for a brief trip to Moscow or St Petersburg, but if you plan to travel elsewhere in Russia and visit more out-of-the-way places, a hire car is recommended.

If you intend to bring your own vehicle into Russia, you must arrange your trip at least six weeks in advance. Details of cars must be entered on your visa. Motorists who present their national driving licence at the border will be asked to complete a driving licence insert so that the information on the licence can be understood by the Russian authorities. Visitors who are intending to stay in Russia for longer than a month should obtain an international driving licence. All foreign cars must show a nationality plate. There is now Third Party Liability but the Green Card or international insurance certificate does not apply.

Driving conditions. Roads and traffic conditions in the cities are generally poor, with lots of potholes, tram-tracks, roadworks and congestion. It is also easy to get lost. Speed limits are 60 km/h (37 mph) in built-up areas, 90 km/h (55 mph) on highways; seat belts are compulsory. It is an offence to drive after consuming even one alcoholic drink. The notoriously corrupt traffic police GIBDD, still known by their Soviet-era name GAI, have the right to stop you and impose on-the-spot fines for infringements, and foreign vehicles are a favourite target.

Petrol. Petrol can be bought with either roubles or credit cards. High-grade petrol and diesel are sometimes difficult to find, and unleaded is almost unknown. The standard grade in Russia is 76-octane, but the 95-octane fuel needed by foreign cars is available, though rather expensive. Service stations are usually self-service – pay first, then fill up.

Fluid measures

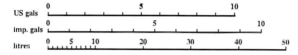

Distance

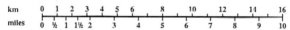

Road signs. Most Russian road signs are the standard international ones, and can be easily understood. Some knowledge of the Cyrillic alphabet (see LANGUAGE) is useful for reading place names, though most routes have signs in the Latin alphabet also.

внимание, впереди ведутся работы	Roadwork in progress
(внимание) пешеходы	(Watch out for) pedestrians

встречное движение	Oncoming traffic
въезд запрещен	No entry
движение в один ряд	Traffic in single lane
держитесь правой стороны	Keep right
камнепад	Falling rocks
конец ограничительной зоны	End of no-passing zone
не задерживаться	No waiting
обгон запрещён	No overtaking (passing)
объезд	Diversion (detour)
ограниченная скорость	Reduce speed
одностороннее движение	One-way traffic
опасно	Danger
опасный поворот	Dangerous bend (curve)
плохая дорога	Bad road surface
светофор за сто метров	Traffic lights at 100 metres
сквозного проезда нет	No through road (dead end road)
стоянка запрещена	No parking
сужение дороги	Bottleneck

International Driving Licence	(международные) водительские права	*(mezhdunarodniye) voitel'skiye prava*
Car registration papers	техпаспорт автомобиля	*tekhpasport avtomobilya*
Intourist vouchers	талоны Интуриста	*taloni inturista*
Are we on the right road for …?	Мы правильно едем в …?	*mi pravil' no yedem v*
Check the oil/ tires/battery.	Проверьте масло/ давление в шинах/ аккумулятор	*prover'te maslo/ davleniye v shinakh/ akkumulyator*
I've broken down.	У меня авария.	*u menya avariya*

There's been an accident.	**Произошла авария.**	*proizoshla avariya*

Breakdown. In the event of an accident or breakdown, seek help from the traffic police (GIBDD). Remember that spare parts for foreign cars may have to be ordered from abroad, and this can take a long time. You are strongly recommended to take out emergency breakdown coverage in your own country before leaving.

E

ELECTRICITY (электричество–*elektrichestvo*)

Electric current in Russia is mostly 220V/50Hz AC, with European-style round two-pin sockets. Most hotels have 110/220V shaver sockets.

EMBASSIES and CONSULATES
(посольстваж консульства *posol'stav; konsool'stvah*)

British Embassy: Smolenskaya Naberezhnaya 10, Moscow; tel. (095) 956 7200.

Canadian Embassy: Starokonyushenny Pereulok 23, Moscow; tel. (095) 956 6666.

Irish Embassy: Grokholskiy Pereulok 5, Moscow; tel. (095) 288 4101.

US Embassy: Novinskiy Bulvar 15, Moscow; tel. (095) 728 5000.

US Consulate: Ul. Furshtatskaya 15, St Petersburg; tel. (812) 331 2600.

British Consulate: Ul. Proletarskoy Dictatury 5, St Petersburg; tel. (812) 320 3200.

Where's the British/ American Embassy?	**Где английское/ американское посольство?**	*gde angliyskoyel amerikanskoyel posol'stvo*

EMERGENCIES (специальные службы – *spetsial'niye sluzhby*)

Unless you are fluent in Russian, you should seek help through your hotel service desk. If you can speak Russian, the following numbers may be useful:

Fire   01   **Police   02**   **Ambulance   03**

Although we hope you'll never need them, here are a few words you might like to learn in advance:

Careful!	**Осторожно!**	*ostorozhno*
Help!	**Помогите!**	*pomogite*
Police!	**Милиция!**	*militsiya*
Stop!	**Стой!**	*stoy*
Stop thief!	**Держи вора!**	*derzhi vora*

G

GETTING THERE

Travelling to Moscow and St Petersburg from Great Britain

By air. There are direct scheduled flights from London to Moscow daily, and 2–3 days a week to St Petersburg. The best deal is an APEX return ticket, which must be booked 21 days in advance. The cheapest way to fly is to take an inclusive package tour. Travel companies offer a variety of tours which include Moscow and St Petersburg. Ask your travel agent for further details.

By road. It is possible to drive your own vehicle to Russia. There are official entry points into the country from Ukraine, Belarus, Estonia and Finland. Driving from western Europe, the shortest route to Moscow is from either Germany or the Czech Republic through Poland. From the Polish-Belorussian border at Brest one proceeds via Minsk in the Ukraine and Smolensk; to reach St Petersburg, you'll travel via Minsk, Orsha and Vitebsk (in Belorussia), and on to Pskov and St Petersburg. St Petersburg can also be approached by car from Finland – the city is only 218km (135 miles) from the Finnish border. (See also DRIVING).

By rail. It is possible to travel to Moscow by train, first crossing the Channel to Ostend, then continuing via Brussels, Cologne, Düsseldorf, Hannover, Berlin, Warsaw and Brest, picking up frequent onward connections to St Petersburg. The journey to Moscow takes about 2 days, and to St Petersburg an additional 7 to 9 hours.

By sea. Ask your travel agent for details of Baltic cruises, which depart from London and call at the major Baltic ports, including St Petersburg. If you are travelling to Russia via Scandinavia, it is possible to take a ferry to St Petersburg from either Stockholm in Sweden or Helsinki in Finland (summer months only).

From the US

By air. Direct scheduled flights depart from New York for Moscow daily. You can also fly direct to Moscow from several other major American cities. The cheapest way is to book an inclusive package tour through a specialist travel agency.

GUIDES and TOURS

Official guides are provided as part of all package holidays. In both cities, there are many independent tour operators available for guided tours and sightseeing trips. Ask at your hotel front desk for more details.

HEALTH and MEDICAL CARE (медицинское обслуживание – *obsluzhivaniye;* see also EMERGENCIES)

Make sure you take out adequate medical insurance before leaving for Russia, and that you are covered for an emergency evacuation flight home. Medical services are available free to British citizens in state-run hospitals. The following private clinics are also available:

In Moscow: American Medical Center, 2-Tverskaya Yamskaya 10, tel. (095) 956 3366; European Medical Centre Group, Spiridonievsky Pereulok 5, tel. (095) 933-6655, <www.emcmos.ru>. In St Petersburg: American Medical Center, 10 Serpukhovskaya Ulitsa, tel. (812) 326 6272; American Medical Clinic, Nagerezhnaya Reki Moiki 78, tel. (812) 140 2090, <www.amclinic.com>; British-American Family Practice, Grafsky Pereulok 7, tel. (812) 327 6030, <www.british--americanclinic.com>. For minor ailments a doctor can be called through your hotel service desk. There may be a small charge for pre-scriptions. All sorts of Western medicines are available in the shops.

No vaccinations are compulsory for travel to Russia, but for longer visits it may be advisable to have a diphtheria booster.

a doctor	**доктор**	*doktor*
an ambulance	**скорая помощь**	*skoraya pomoshch'*
hospital	**больница**	*bol'nitsa*
an upset stomach	**расстройство желудка**	*rasstroystvo zheludka*
chills	**простуда**	*prostuda*
a fever	**жар**	*zhar*

HOLIDAYS (праздничные дни–*prazdnichiye dni*)

31 December–2 January	New Year
7 January	Russian Orthodox Christmas
23 February	Day of the Defender of the Motherland
8 March	International Women's Day
1–2 May	Labour Day/ Spring Festival
9 May	Victory Day
12 June	Russian Independence Day
7 November	Day of Reconciliation
12 December	Russian Constitution Day

Are you open tomorrow?	**Вы открыты завтра?** vi *otkriti zavtra*

L

LANGUAGE

The Russian language may seem like a daunting obstacle to communication, but it need not be a problem. All organisations that cater to foreign tourists have at least a few English-speaking staff members. In Moscow and St Petersburg many people can speak a little English, but your stay is likely to be more enjoyable and rewarding if you learn a few basic words for hello, goodbye, please, and thank you.

As for the Cyrillic alphabet: if it's all Greek to you, that's hardly surprising, as it is derived from the Greek alphabet. It is not difficult to learn, however, and it is of great help in finding your way around if you are able to read signs with street names and the names of Metro stations.

The alphabet is shown below. The first and second columns show the printed letters, capitals and lower case. The third column shows you approximately what the Cyrillic letters correspond to in English, and is the basis for the simplified transliteration used in this guide.

The letter ь, shown below as an apostrophe ('), gives a 'soft' pronunciation to the preceding consonant. A similar effect can be produced by pronouncing y as in yet – but very, very short – after the consonant.

А	а	a	Р	р	r
Б	б	b	С	с	s
В	в	v	Т	т	t
Г	г	g	У	у	u
Д	д	d	Ф	ф	f
Е	е	e-ye	Х	х	kh
Ё	ё	yo	Ц	ц	ts
Ж	ж	zh	Ч	х	ch

З з	z	Ш ш	sh
И и	i	Щ щ	shch
Й й	j	– ь	'(mute)
К к	k	– ы	y
Л л	l	– ъ	(mute)
М м	m	ý э	eh
Н н	n	Ю ю	yu
О о	o	Я я	ya
П п	p		

LOST PROPERTY (пропажи и находки – *propazhi i nakhodki*)

Ask for advice from your hotel reception before contacting the police. For items left behind on public transport you might ask the hotel to telephone the head office of the Metro or bus company, but don't hold out too much hope.

I've lost my wallet/ handbag (female).	**Я потерял(а) бумажник/сумку.**	*ya poteryal(a) bumazhnik/sumku*

MAPS (планы; карты – *plany; karty*)

The fall of the old Soviet Union has led to many streets and places having their pre-Revolutionary names restored. This means that street maps published before 1991 can be rather confusing.

If you need a more detailed city map than those in this guide, you will find up-to-date maps in English at bookstands in the bigger hotels. A good one is *The New Moscow City Map and Guide,* published by the American company Northern Cartographic. The Falk-Verlag street plans of Moscow and St Petersburg are also useful.

a street plan of …	**план …**	*plan*
a road map of this region	**карта дорог этого района**	*karta dorog etovo rayona*

MEDIA

Radio and TV (радио; телевидение–*radio; televideniye*). Most hotels now offer satellite television in individual rooms, with CNN, MTV and sports and movie channels available. If you have a short-wave radio, you can pick up the BBC World Service, SW 12,095 and 15,070 MHz, and Voice of America, SW 15 and 6,866 MHz. Radio 7 (FM 73.4 and 104.7) broadcasts news in English on the half hour.

Newspapers and magazines (газеты; журналы–*gazeti; zhurnali*). Locally produced English-language publications include the daily *Moscow Times* (free), and the bi-monthly *Moscow Magazine* (US $5), both of which provide coverage of news and features, restaurant reviews, and entertainment listings.

In St Petersburg you can get the monthly *Neva News,* the bi-weekly *St Petersburg Times,* and *Pulse,* a monthly magazine. All three publications are free. American and British magazines and newspapers can be bought from the bookshops in the big hotels, and there are also plenty of English language bookstores, including Anglia British Bookshop, Khlebbny Pereulok 2/3, and American Bookstore, Denezhnyy Pereulok 8/10 (both in Moscow) and Anglia Bookshop, Fontanka 42 (in St Petersburg.

Have you any English-language newspapers?	Есть ли у вас какие-нибудь газеты на английском языке?	*yest'li u vas kakiy enibud' gazety na angliyskam yazikye*

MONEY MATTERS

Currency. The unit of currency is the *rouble* (рубли). In 1998, the central bank removed three zeros from the old currency and began issuing new notes and coins as it withdrew the old. The new rouble denominations are as follows: banknotes of 5, 10, 100, 500 and 1,000 roubles, and coins of 5, 10, and 50 kopeks and 1, 2 and 5 roubles. Notes dated before 1998 are no longer legal tender.

From 1 January 1994 it has been illegal to conduct cash transactions in foreign currency within Russia. Hard currency transactions can, however, be carried out by bank transfer and charge and credit cards.

There is no limit to the amount of foreign currency allowed to be brought into Russia. However, all money taken into the country (including travellers cheques) must be declared upon entering the country. Currency may be exchanged in any amount at banks, licensed exchange offices and at many department stores and shops. Exchange rates between the rouble and hard currencies are set by authorised Russian banks. However, rates of exchange can vary greatly, so shop around.

Banks and currency exchange offices. The Russian banking system is currently struggling to join the 21st century, and cannot yet provide the services taken for granted in the West, but it has made great strides in the last few years. Hard currency can be changed into roubles in most hotels, at airports, and at currency exchange bureaus, which are plentiful. You will need your passport and your customs declaration form.

Travellers cheques, credit cards and ATMs. Travellers cheques can be exchanged at all banks and major hotels, but a large commission may apply. The American Express office is located on Sadovaya-Kudrinskaya Street 21a, in Moscow and at the Grand Hotel Europe in St Petersburg.

The use of credit cards is spreading. Major credit cards (American Express, Diners Club, Eurocard/Mastercard, Visa International) are widely accepted.

ATMs are generously distributed in both Moscow and St Petersburg, so it's easy to get cash advances in roubles on your credit/debit card.

Do you accept travellers cheques?	**Вы берёте дорожные чекн?**	*vi beryote dorozhnye cheki*
Can I pay with this credit card?	**Можно платить по этой кредитной карточке?**	*mozhno platit' po etoj kreditnoj kartochke*

OPENING TIMES

Banks are generally open for foreign exchange 9.30am to 5pm Monday to Friday.

Currency exchange offices in hotels are open longer than banks, usually 9am to 9pm.

The Kremlin in Moscow is open daily 10am to 7pm (5pm October to April), closed Thursday.

Lenin's Mausoleum is open 10am to 1pm (3pm on Sunday), and is closed Monday and Friday.

Museums and art galleries have no standard opening times, but are usually open between 10am and 6pm. They are generally closed one day a week, often Monday, and on the last Wednesday, Thursday, or Friday of the month. In Moscow, the **Pushkin Museum of Fine Arts** is open 10am to 7pm, closed Monday, and the **Tretyakov Art Gallery** is open 10am to 7pm, closed Monday. In St Petersburg, the **Hermitage** opens 10.30am to 6pm (10.30am to 5pm on Sundays), closed Monday.

Post offices are open 9am to 9pm, and close for lunch from 2 to 3pm.

Restaurants are usually open noon to 11pm, though newer, café/bistro style places may open earlier and close later.

Opening hours for **shops** vary widely, but are typically 10am to 9pm for department stores, and 9am to 8pm for food shops, with a lunch break of 1 to 2pm or 2 to 3pm.

PHOTOGRAPHY (фотография – *fotografiya*)

Western brands of film are available, although you may want to bring supplies with you just in case. New photo shops are beginning to spring up in the city centres. One-hour photo processing is available at the Fuji shop, Novy Arbat 25, Moscow, and at Yarky Mir, Nevskij Prospekt 6, St Petersburg.

With the passing of the Soviet Union, restrictions on photography are no longer so strictly enforced, but it is still forbidden to take pictures from aircraft over Russian territory, or of military facilities and border zones. Many museums and art galleries forbid flash and tripod, and some charge a fee for the use of a camera.

May we take a picture…?	**Можно сфотографировать…?**	*mozhno sfata grafirovat'*
of this/of you	**это/вас**	*eto/vas*
I'd like a film for this camera	**Мне нужна пленка для этого аппарата.**	*mne nuzhna plyonka dlya etovo apparata*
How long will it take to develop (and print) this?	**Сколько нужно времени, чтобы проявить (и напечатать)?**	*skol'ko nuzhno vremeni shtobi proyavit' (i napechatat')*

POLICE (милиция–*militsiya*)

The only policemen you are likely to see are the traffic patrolmen (GIBDD), who police major streets and intersections, waving down cars with their black-and-white striped batons, and administering on-the-spot fines. If you find yourself having to deal with the police, few of whom speak English, ask for assistance from your hotel service desk.

Where is the nearest police station?	**Где ближайшее отделение милиции?**	*gde blizhaysheye otdeleniye militsii*

POST OFFICES (почта; телеграф–*pochta; telegraf*)

Almost all hotels have their own postal kiosks, where you can buy stamps and send parcels, telegrams, and faxes. The main international post offices in Moscow (Varshavskoe Shosse 37a) and St Petersburg (Pochtamtskaya Ulitsa 9) handle stamps, express mail, parcels, faxes, and philately, and are open 9am to 9pm, closed 2 to 3pm.

General delivery. The Russian postal system is slow and inefficient, with both incoming and outgoing international mail taking up to three weeks. Courier services such as DHL and Fedex are the only speedy and reliable method for important mail. American Express cardholders can have mail sent to the Amex offices in Moscow and St Petersburg (for locations, see MONEY MATTERS).

express	**нарочным**	*narochnym*
airmail	**авиа**	*avia*
registered	**заказное**	*zakaznoye*
poste restante (general delivery)	**до востребования**	*do vostrebovaniya*
A stamp for this letter/postcard, please.	**Марку для этого письма/открытки, пожалуйста.**	*marku dlya etovo pis'ma/otkritki pozhalusta*

R

RELIGION

The Russian Orthodox Church is now emerging from the dark ages of Soviet oppression, when all forms of religious worship were banned. Many confiscated church buildings have been returned to the church and are being restored to their former glory.

Moscow and St Petersburg are home to people of many different religious denominations and places of worship, including Catholic, Protestant, and Anglican churches. For information about services, see the Thursday edition of the *Moscow Times,* or ask at your hotel's service desk.

T

TELEPHONE (телефон – *telefon*)

The Russian telephone system is hopelessly overburdened, and making a domestic call is often a frustrating process involving busy lines and wrong numbers. Local calls made from your hotel are no longer free. New public phones that take phonecards (sold in Metro stations, post offices, and banks) have replaced the old token-operated payphones. These new cardphones can be used for local, intercity, and international calls. This is the cheapest way to call abroad. Direct international calls are expensive.

Fast, easy, and reliable (but very expensive) are the satellite phone booths that are now to be found in most tourist hotels. These operate with a prepaid phone card or major credit card, and allow you to dial direct to anywhere in the world. Instructions in English are clearly displayed, as are rates per minute.

Country Direct service is now available in Russia. This is mainly useful for calling the US and involves a toll-free number in Russia that connects you to an operator from ATT, Sprint, or MCI. Canada has a similar service. Check with your phone company for access numbers.

TIME ZONES

Moscow and St Petersburg are 3 hours ahead of GMT. Daylight saving time is in operation between 31 March and 30 September when clocks are put forward 1 hour. The following chart gives the times in major cities round the world when it is noon in Moscow.

Los Angeles	Chicago	New York	London	**Moscow**
1am	3am	4am	9am	**noon**

TIPPING

Tipping, once officially discouraged, is now accepted practice in Russia. Reckon on 10 to 15 percent for waiters and waitresses (unless a service charge has been included in the bill). Tour guides and hotel maids also appreciate a tip, or a small gift of cigarettes, toiletries, or sweets.

TOILETS/RESTROOMS (туалет–*tualet*)

Public toilets in Moscow and St Petersburg are often dirty, smelly, and lacking toilet paper. Clean toilets can be found in hotels, art galleries, and museums. They are marked M (мужской–*muzhskoy*) for men, and Ж (женский–*zhenskiy*) for women.

TOURIST INFORMATION OFFICES

While planning your trip, it might be useful to contact the Russian National Tourist Offices in your home country:

Canada: Russian National Tourist Office
1801 McGill College Avenue, Suite 630,
Montreal, Quebec H3A 2N4; tel. (514) 849 6394.

UK: Russian National Tourist Office
70 Piccadilly, London W1J 8HP
tel. (020) 7495 7555; <www.visitrussia.org.uk>.

US: Russian National Group
130 West 42nd Street, Suite 412, New York, NY 10036
tel. (212) 575 3431 or (877) 221 7120 (toll-free in US);
<www.russia-travel.com>.
(Represents the Russian National Tourist Office and the Russian Association of Travel Agencies (RATA).

Ask at your hotel, and also try the English-language newspapers (see MEDIA). They are free and contain plenty of useful information.

Intourist (<www.intourist.com>), the former state travel agency, was privatised in 1993. Although it no longer has a monopoly on Russian travel, it continues to offer services in all the larger Russian cities and, with its huge network of offices and agents, remains the largest travel company in the country. Besides group tours, Intourist also arranges for individual journeys to Russia. Intourist has no representation in the US; in the UK it can be contacted at:

> 7 Wellington Terrace, Notting Hill, London W2 4LW;
> tel. (020) 7727 4100 or (0870) 112 1232 (reservation line);
> <www.intourist.co.uk>. There are also offices in Glasgow
> and Manchester.

TRANSPORT

Buses and trams (автобус; трамвай – *avtobus*; *tram*). Moscow and St Petersburg are served by an extensive network of bus, trolley bus, and tram routes, which run from about 6am to 1am. You can buy tickets (талон – *talon*), in strips of five or ten, from street kiosks, and occasionally from the driver. When you board, you validate your ticket in one of the hand-punches above the seats. Stops are quite far apart, and marked by signs with A for buses, and T or 'трам' for trams. Ask at your hotel which number bus you need for a particular destination. Unfortunately, buses are very crowded, infrequent, and unreliable.

Metro (метро – *metro*). The Moscow Metro (underground railway) is the city's pride and joy. Many stations are magnificently decorated, and the trains are fast, clean, and frequent; you will rarely have to wait more than 2 minutes. Trains run from 6am to 1am, getting very crowded during the morning and evening rush hour, and at lunch time. You buy a metro card at the cashier's desk (касса – *kassa*), and place it in the slot at the entrance barrier. When the light changes from red to green, you can pass. One fare takes you anywhere on the network. If you don't want to get lost, you should learn the Cyrillic alphabet *(see pages 115–116)* so that you can read the names of the stations and follow signs at interchange stations. You can get by on short trips by counting stops, and following the crowds to the exit. The St Petersburg Metro works the same way, but has a less extensive network.

станция метро	Metro station
касса/кассы	ticket office
(нет) вход(а)	(No) entrance
(нет) выход(а)	(No) exit
переход	interchange
на станцию ...	to the ... station
на линию ...	to the ... line
выход в город	exit to street
к поездам	to the trains
от себя	push
к себе	pull

Trains (поезд – *poyezd*). Moscow is linked by rail to most parts of Russia and to Western Europe. Trains are slow but comfortable, and a relaxing means of travel. There are 15 trains a day between Moscow and St Petersburg, and the journey takes between 4 and 8½ hours. Sleepers can be arranged in Moscow; tel. (095) 921 4513 for rail information in English.

Taxis (такси – *taksi*). Official taxis are identified by a green light in the windscreen, and a chequered pattern on the side. City centre taxi ranks are marked by a sign bearing the letter T. You must negotiate a fare before you get into the taxi; meters are installed but rarely used. If you try to hail a taxi in the street, you will often find that ordinary cars will stop; these are private citizens trying to make a little extra money. Again, if you can speak Russian, you might be able to negotiate a fare. But never get into a car or taxi alone if there is someone else apart from the driver inside; you may be mugged. Your hotel can telephone for a reliable private taxi, and quote a price (in hard currency) for your journey. Book your taxi at least an hour in advance. The major hotels have their own chauffeured cars, which are safer and less hassle than street taxis.

WEIGHTS and MEASURES
(For distance and fluid charts see DRIVING)

Length

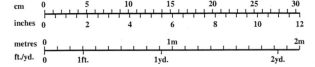

Weight

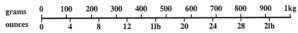

Temperature

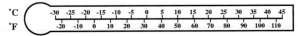

YOUTH HOSTELS

Russia now has a Youth Hostel Association (RYHA) affiliated with the International Youth Hostelling Association. RYHA offers clean and inexpensive hostel accommodation up to Western standards. In addition, many of its youth hostels offer visa support and have their own budget travel agencies. Contact your national YHA, or email RYHA at: ryh@ryh.spb.ru (see also ACCOMMODATION for more information).

SOME USEFUL EXPRESSIONS

where/when/how	где/когда/как	*gde/kogda/kdk*
how long/how far	сколько/как далеко	*skol'ko/kak daleko*
yesterday/today/ tomorrow	вчера/сегодня/ завтра	*vchera/sevodnya/ zavtra*
left/right	левыйё/равый	*leviy/praviy*
up/down	вверх/вниз	*vverkh/vniz*
good/bad	хороший/плохой	*khoroshiy/plokhoy*
hot/cold	горячий/холодный	*goryachiy/kholodniy*
open/closed	открытый/закрытый	*otkriotiy/zakritiy*

Numbers

1	один	*odin*
2	два	*dva*
3	три	*tri*
4	четыре	*chetyre*
5	пять	*pyat'*
6	шесть	*shest'*
7	семь	*sem'*
8	восемь	*vosem'*
9	девять	*devyat'*
10	десять	*desyat'*
11	одиннадцать	*odinnatsat'*
12	двенадцать	*dvenatsat*
13	тринадцать	*trinatsat'*
14	четырнадцать	*chetirnatsat'*
15	пятнадцать	*pyatnatsat'*
16	шестнадцать	*shestnatsat'*
17	семнадцать	*semnatsat'*
18	восемнадцать	*vosemnatsat'*
19	девятнадцать	*devyatnatsat'*
20	двадцать	*dvatsat'*
21	двадцать один	*dvatsat' odin*
22	двадцать два	*dvatsat' dva*

30	**тридцать**	*tritsat'*
40	**сорок**	*sorok*
50	**пятьдесят**	*pyat'desyat*
60	**шестьдесят**	*shest'desyat*
70	**семьдесят**	*sem'desyat*
80	**восемьдесят**	*vosem'desyat*
90	**девяносто**	*devyanosto*
100	**сто**	*sto*
101	**сто один**	*sto odin*
102	**сто два**	*sto dva*
500	**пятьсот**	*pyatsot*
1,000	**тысяча**	*tysyacha*

Days of the Week

Sunday	**воскресенье**	*voskresenye*
Monday	**понедельник**	*ponedyel'nik*
Tuesday	**вторник**	*vtornik*
Wednesday	**среда**	*sreda*
Thursday	**четверг**	*chetverg*
Friday	**пятница**	*pyatnitsa*
Saturday	**суббота**	*subbota*

Months of the Year

January	**январь**	*yanvar'*
February	**февраль**	*fevral'*
March	**март**	*mart*
April	**апрель**	*aprel'*
May	**май**	*mai*
June	**июнь**	*iyun'*
July	**июль**	*iyul'*
August	**август**	*avgust*
September	**сентябрь**	*sentyabr'*
October	**октябрь**	*oktyabr'*
November	**ноябрь**	*noyabr'*
December	**декабрь**	*dekabr'*

Recommended Hotels

The hotel scene in Moscow and St Petersburg is currently undergoing a major shake-up following the collapse of the Soviet Union. Western hotel management groups are entering into joint ventures with Intourist and other Russian partners, with the aim of raising the quality of service and efficiency to levels comparable with those in the West. Many joint venture hotels are now operating. This means greater freedom of choice for travellers, who until now have had little or no say in choosing their accommodation, simply accepting whatever Intourist offered. The selection listed below includes both JV hotels and older Intourist establishments.

As a basic guide we have used the symbols below to indicate the price per night for a double room with bath, including breakfast:

$	under $80
$$	$80–150
$$$	$150–280
$$$$	over $280

Unless otherwise indicated, assume that all establishments accept major credit cards.

MOSCOW

Aerostar $$$ *Leningradskij Prospekt 37, korpus 9; tel. (095) 213 9000, fax (095) 213 9001; <www.aerostar.ru>.* Comfortable four-star hotel at city air terminal, only four Metro stops from city centre. 2 restaurants, 2 bars and a business centre. 343 rooms.

Akademicheskaya I $ *Donskaya Ulitsa 1; tel. (095) 238 4161, fax (095) 237 2539.* Located near Gorky Park; formerly used for visiting scholars. 700 rooms, mainly used by students and faculty.

Arbat $$ *Plotnikov Pereulok 12; tel. (095) 244 7635, fax (095) 244 7635.* This small hotel has modern services, but it retains a strong Soviet feel; wonderful location in the Old Arbat area.

Belgrade $–$$ *Smolenskaya Ploshchad 8; tel. (095) 248 2841/2041, fax (095) 248 2814.* Tower block on Garden Ring, near the Arbat. Rooms are small, clean, and reasonably comfortable, with shower, WC, and television. Restaurant. 443 rooms. Mastercard and Visa only.

Baltschug Kempinski $$$$ *Ulitsa Baltchug 1; tel. (095) 230 6500, fax (095) 230 6502; <www.kempinskimoscow.com>.* A fine hotel reconstructed within the 1898 neoclassical façade of the former Hotel Bucharest. Located in the Zamoskvorechye district just across the Moskva River, it enjoys splendid views of Red Square and the Kremlin. 232 luxuriously appointed rooms.

Heritage Hostel $ *Ulitsa Kosmonavtov 2; tel. (095) 975 3501, fax (095) 975 3601, email evgen@az-tour.msk.ru.* A typical youth hostel—basic rooms at low prices (ranging from $18 per person to $40 for a private double). English-speaking staff can assist you with visa and travel arrangements.

Holiday Inn $$ *Dmitrovskoye Shosse 171; tel. 937 0670; fax 937 0671; <www.himv.da.ru>.* Located in pleasant surroundings at the city's edge, 15 minutes from Sheremetyevo International Airport and 40 minutes from downtown Moscow, this hotel has good-value accommodation. 154 well-equipped rooms.

Kosmos $$$ *Prospekt Mira 150; tel. (095) 234 1000, fax (095) 215 8880; <www.hotelcosmos.ru>.* A huge, curved skyscraper built in 1980 for the Moscow Olympics. Standard Intourist hotel, but with a swimming pool. A 20-minute Metro ride from the city centre. 1707 rooms, 60 suites.

Leningradskaya $$ *Kalanchovskaya Ulitsa 21/40; tel. (095) 975 3032, fax (095) 975 4943*. Large Moscow hotel catering to business people. Offers all applicable amenities such as currency exchange, conference facilities, and travel centre. 300 rooms.

Marco Polo Presnaya $$$ *Spiridonyevskij Pereulok 9; tel. (095) 244 3631, fax (095) 926 5402; <www.presnja.ru>*. Small, quality hotel in a quiet street near Pushkin Square. Furnished in traditional Russian style. Local and international cuisine; 68 rooms. Translation service and business centre.

Metropol $$$–$$$$ *Teatralnyj Proezd 1; tel. (095) 927 6000, fax (095) 927 6010; <www.metropol-moscow.ru>*. A renovated, turn-of-the-20th-century classic: Art-Nouveau decor and a glass-roofed ballroom. Good restaurants, café, and the Artists' Bar.

Mezhdunarodnaya $$$ *12 Krasnopresnenskaya, Naberezhnaya; tel. (095) 253 2287; <www.hotel.wtcmoscow.ru>*. This large hotel is an integral part of WTC Moscow, and has a shopping mall, a variety of restaurants, a swimming pool, and sauna. One of Moscow's best hotels. 484 rooms

National $$$$ *Mokhovaya Ulitsa 15/1; tel. (095) 258 7000, <www.national.ru>*. Fine, centrally located hotel. Restaurant, bar, comprehensive business facilities. 230 rooms

Novotel $$$ *Sheremetyevo II Airport; tel. (095) 926 5900, fax (095) 926 5903*. A typical airport hotel that provides the usual conveniences of other Novotel hotels. 500 rooms

Radisson SAS Slavjanskaya $$$$ *Berezhkovskaya Naberezhnaya 2; tel. (095) 941 8020, fax (095) 941 8000; <www.radisson.com>*. Intourist/Radisson joint venture, with 430 rooms, by Kievskaya Metro station. Café, three restaurants, health club.

Renaissance $$$–$$$$ *Olympiyskij Prospekt 18/1; tel. (095) 931 9000, fax (095) 931 9076; <www.renaissancehotels.com>.* A German-Russian joint venture, famous for Sunday brunch in the glass-domed dining room, amid waterfalls and lush greenery. 476 rooms, 12 suites.

Savoy $$$ *Ulitsa Rozhdestvenka 3; tel. (095) 929 8555, fax (095) 230 2186.* One of Moscow's best hotels – opened in 1912 and now restored (and newly renovated in 2004). Murals, gilt trim, top-class service, and an ideal location– a block from the Bolshoi or 5 minutes from Red Square. Business centre, casino; 86 rooms.

Sheraton Palace Hotel $$$$ *Ulitsa 1-ya Tverskaya-Yamskaya 19; tel. (095) 931 9700, fax (095) 931 9708; <www.sheratonpalace.ru>.* A new joint venture just a short Metro trip from Red Square. Well-furnished rooms; three restaurants, bar, and health club. 218 rooms. Breakfast not included.

Sovietskaya $$$ *Leningradskij Prospekt 32; tel. (095) 250 7253, fax (095) 250 8003.* This hotel is unique, in that it has room service. Winston Churchill stayed here. Recently renovated and better than ever. 100 rooms.

Ukraina $–$$ *Kutuzovskij Prospekt 2/1; tel. (095) 243 3030, fax (095) 956 2078.* A good old Intourist offering, in an impressive 1950s Gothic skyscraper. The 436 rooms are old but spacious. Major credit cards. The food leaves a lot to be desired, but never fear, Pizza Hut is just down the street.

ST PETERSBURG

Angleterre Hotel $$$ *Bolshaya Morskaya Ulitsa 39; tel. (812) 313 5666; fax. 313 5125; <www.angleterrehotel.com>.* This completely refurbished hotel managed by the Rocco Forte group has 193 beautifully designed bedrooms, the stylish

Borsalino Brasserie offering contemporary European food, a conference and business centre, fully equipped fitness centre with sauna and small pool, plus a nightclub and casino.

Astoria $$$ *Ulitsa Bolshaya Morskaya 39; tel. (812) 313 5757, fax (812) 313 5134; <www.roccofortehotels.com>.* Sister hotel to, and next door to, the Angleterre, this grand hotel dating from 1912 has been completely renovated. Parquet-floored rooms, four restaurants, two bars, hard currency shop, health club, international newsagent. 188 rooms.

Baltic Star Hotel $$$ *Beriozovaya Alley 3, Strelna; tel. (812) 438 5700; fax (812) 438 5888.* New hotel built in the style of a Russian mansion, in the southern suburbs of the city on the Gulf of Finland. 106 rooms; cottages also available.

Corinthia Nevskij Palace $$$$ *Nevskij Prospekt 57; tel. (812) 380 2001, fax (812) 380 1937; <www.corinthia.ru>.* Renovated by an Austrian joint venture: comfortable, with shops, restaurants, health club. 285 rooms. A 25-minute walk from the Winter Palace.

Dostoyevsky $$ *Vladimirsky Prospect 19; tel. (812) 331 3200; fax (812) 331 3201.* This modern hotel occupies the top floors of the Vladimirsky passage, combining outstanding location and design with memorable service. Conference hall, fitness centre. 207 rooms and suites.

Grand Hotel Europe $$$$ *Ulitsa Mikhailovskaya 1/7; tel. (812) 329 6000, fax (812) 329 6001; <www.grandhotel europe.com>.* A recently modernised Swedish-Russian joint venture and the city's best hotel. 301 bright rooms, satellite TV, 24-hour room service, six restaurants, nightclub, health club.

Breakfast not included. Excellent location off Nevskiy Prospekt and close to the Winter Palace.

International Hostel Holiday $ *Ulitsa Mikhajlova 195009; tel. (812) 327 1070, fax (812) 327 1033; <www.hostel.ru>.* Clean, comfortable rooms plus a snack bar, kitchen and common room. Offers visa support. English-speaking staff.

Moskva $–$$ *Ploshchad Aleksandra Nevskogo 2; tel. (812) 274 0022, fax (812) 274 2130; <www.hotel-moscow.ru>.* A huge building, especially popular with group tours. 770 small but adequate rooms, and poor service by Western standards. Breakfast included. On the River Neva, a 15-minute Metro ride from the city centre.

Pulkovskaya $–$$ *Ploshchad Pobedy 1; tel. (812) 140 3900, fax 140 4311; <www.pulkovskaya.spb.ru>.* Offers a refreshing choice of restaurants and cafés from an otherwise typical Intourist hotel.

Radisson SAS Royal Hotel $$$$ *Nevsky Prospect 49; tel. (812) 322 5000; fax (812) 322 5002; <www.stpetersburg. radissonsas.com>.* Completely renovated hotel encased in historic façade dating from 1730, located on St Petersburg's main boulevard. All modern business facilities. 164 rooms.

St Petersburg $–$$ *Naberezhnaya Pirogovskaya 5/2; tel. (812) 542 9123.* Soviet-style hotel located opposite the cruiser Aurora, with good views. Two restaurants, three nightclubs, two swimming pools, sauna and sports hall. 400 rooms; breakfast included.

St Petersburg International Hostel $ *3-ya Sovetskaya Ulitsa 28, 193036; tel. (812) 329 8018, fax (812) 329 8019; <www.ryh.ru>.* Clean, comfortable rooms. Offers visa support and has its own budget travel agency. Cyber café and library. English-speaking staff.

Recommended Restaurants

Eating out in Moscow and St Petersburg is – well – different. Most traditional restaurants cater to parties out for a wild night on the town, with loud music, dancing, and lots of alcohol. Places where you can simply wander in off the street, order a meal, and be out in an hour or so are few and far between. The choice has traditionally been between good food and service at exorbitant prices, or poor food and terrible service for next to nothing. However, the situation has improved in the wake of liberalisation, with new co-ops and joint ventures opening all the time. The days of cheap eating are almost gone, but Moscow in particular has a varied menu to cater to all tastes and whims. There are useful restaurant listings and reviews in *Moscow Magazine*, *Moscow Times*, and *St Petersburg News* (see MEDIA on page 117). Below is a list of restaurants recommended by Berlitz; if you find other places worth a mention, we'd like to hear from you.

Reservations are necessary unless indicated otherwise. As a basic guide we have used the following symbols to give some idea of the cost of a three-course meal for two. The prices are a US dollar average, with drinks:

$	under $20
$$	$20–40
$$$	$40–70
$$$$	over $70

MOSCOW

Aleksandr Blok $$ *MS Aleksandr Blok, Krasnopresnenskaya Naberezhnaya 12; tel. (095) 255 9284.* Seafood and vegetarian restaurant aboard the hotel ship Alexander Blok. Shark, swordfish, and lobster arrive daily from the Med. Bouzouki music; buffet 7–10:30pm Thursday. Casino attached.

Amadeus $ *Berezhkovskaya Naberezhnaya 2; tel. (095) 941 8020.* A Viennese sidewalk cafe in Moscow. Light dining; open for breakfast, lunch, and dinner.

Baku-Livan $$–$$$ *Ulitsa Tverskaya 24; tel. (095) 299 8506.* Plush Azerbaijani/Lebanese restaurant, serving delicious Middle-Eastern cuisine. Very popular, and tends to be crowded, with a loud and smoky section. Also has a take-away shop good for lunchtime kebabs.

Café Margarita $ *Ulitsa Malaya Bronnaya 28.* A charming eatery, with wooden floor and green-painted tables. Serves tasty local food and rich pastries. Russian menu only. Bring your own alcohol. No reservations.

Expedition $$ *Pevshesky Pereulok 6; tel. (095) 917 9510.* One of the few original Siberian restaurants. Fine fish and meat dishes.

Farkhad $ *Bolshaya Marfinskaya 4; tel. (095) 218 4136.* Highly recommended Russian restaurant serving Azerbaijani cuisine. No credit cards.

Glazour $$$–$$$$ *Smolenskij Bul'var 12/19; tel. (095) 248 4438.* Luxurious Russian and European joint venture serving quality Russian dishes such as aubergine caviar and elk stew.

Kitezh $$ *Petrovskaya Ulitsa, 23/10; tel. (095) 209 6685.* Russian village-style interior, well-known for its vegetarian menu. Music and shows in evenings.

Kommersant $$ *Pokrovskaya Ulitsa, 33/22; tel. (095) 924 4071.* This eatery is owned by the publisher who prints the famous

Kommersant business newspaper, making this a Moscow landmark to experience.

Kropotkinskaya, 36 $$$ *Ulitsa Prechistenka, 36; tel. (095) 201 7500.* Moscow's first co-op restaurant, and still one of the best. Two dining rooms – formal upstairs, cosy downstairs. Classic Russian cuisine. Reserve a few days ahead.

Mei-Hua $$ *1 Stroyenie, Ulitsa Rusakovskaya 2/1; tel. (095) 264 9574.* Renowned as the best Chinese restaurant in Moscow; the cuisine here is superb. No credit cards.

Onegin $$ *Prichistenka Ulitsa 12, tel. (095) 201 4294.* Stylish, yet casual and quiet place serving Russian and European cuisine.

Pushkin Café $$-$$$ *Tverskoi Boulevard, 26a; tel (095) 229 5590.* Totally new recreation of an old Moscow building, with 19th-century interiors; among one of most fashionable places in the city, and open 24 hours with a breakfast menu.

Savoy $$$$ *Savoy Hotel, Ulitsa Rozhdestvenka 3; tel. (095) 929 8600.* Credit cards only. Elegant dining amidst carefully restored Art-Nouveau decor. The atmosphere is formal, the service first class, and the French/Russian cuisine is simply exquisite.

Slavyansky Bazar $$ *Ulitsa Nikolskaya 13; tel. (095) 921 1872.* Established in 1870 and once the haunt of the 19th-century Moscow intelligentsia, this is now a state-run restaurant with floor show, live music, dancing, and champagne and vodka. Fun for parties, but not really the ideal spot for an - intimate *tête-à-tête*.

Stanislavskogo 2 $$-$$$ *Ulitsa Stanislavskogo 2; tel. (095) 291 8689.* A truly great restaurant with a pleasant atmosphere.

Dine on Russian specialties while listening to classical music. No credit cards, roubles only.

U Pirosmani $$$ *Novodevichij Proezd 4; tel. (095) 247 1926.* Violin and piano play in this very popular Georgian restaurant. The food, which is accompanied by Georgian wines, is spicy and delicious. Window tables have a good view of the 16th-century Novodevichij Convent. Cash only.

Yelki-Palki $ *Bolshaya Dmitrovka 23; tel. (095) 200-0965.* There are six of these bistros in the city, and they offer the best bargains in town.

ST PETERSBURG

Admiralteystvo $$ *Corinthia Nevskij Palace Hotel, Nevskij Pr. 57; tel. (812) 275 2001.* The decor is reminiscent of the hull of a ship. Russian seafood dishes are the speciality.

Akvarel $$$ *Prospect Dobrulyubov, 14a; tel. (812) 320 8600.* Good food, and great view on the embankment; young, fashionable crowd.

Chayka $$$ *Griboedova Kanal 14; tel. (812) 312 4631.* The Chayka ('The Seagull') is a lovely nautical dining room, trimmed with brass and leather, serving typical German and Russian dishes including sausage, pickled herring, goulash and caviar. Open until 3am.

Europe $$$$ *Grand Hotel Europe, Ulitsa Mikhajlovskaya 1/7; tel. (812) 329 6630.* A sumptuous art nouveau dining room. Feast on Russian and European dishes beneath a magnificent stained-glass ceiling. The quality of the food and service are definitely in keeping with the expense-account prices. Try the jazz brunch on Sundays; live music Monday–Friday and dancing on Saturdays.

Golden Dragon $$ *Ulitsa Dekabristov 62, near Mariinsky Theatre; tel. (812) 114 8441.* If you become tired of Russian fare, try this delightful mixture of Chinese and Southeast-Asian cuisines.

Idiot $ *Naberezhnaya Reki Moiki 82; tel. 315 1675.* Great atmosphere, great cappuccino and good vegetarian meals.

Ketino $$ *8th Line 23, Vasilevsky Island; tel. (812) 326 0196.* Exquisite Georgian cooking, but not cheap. Fine collection of Georgian art on display.

Macaroni $$ *Rubinstein Ulitsa 23; tel. (812) 315 6147.* One of the few fine Italian restaurants in the city.

Metropol $$$ *Sadovaya Ulitsa 22; tel. (812) 320 2281.* The oldest restaurant in St. Petersburg and a fabulous place to have lunch. European cuisine.

Molly's Irish Bar $ *Rubinshtejna Ulitsa 36; tel. (812) 319 9768.* Just what St. Petersburg needs, a good Irish pub! Traditional Irish fare, including Irish stew and Guinness on tap.

Nevskiy 40 $–$$ *Nevskij Prospekt 40; tel. (812) 312 2457.* Pleasant, relaxed atmosphere in this German bar-bistro, with wood-panelled walls and brass trim. Soups, pasta, pizza, Chinese dishes, and cakes and pastries.

Nikolai $$$ *Ulitsa Bolshaya Morskaya 52, next to St Isaac's Square; tel. (812) 311 1402.* An elegant restaurant serving European cuisine. They specialise in seafood dishes, using salmon imported fresh from Finland.

Onegin **$$$$** *Sadovaya Ulitsa 11; tel. (812) 311 8384*. Exquisite French and Russian cuisine, and pricey; exclusive club frequented by local celebrities. Late-night DJ.

Russkaya Ribalka **$$** *Uzhnaya Doroga 11; tel. (812) 323 9813*. Offers the best fish dinner and you can even catch your own fish in their pond! Far from the centre, located on the Krestovsky Island on the Petrograd Side.

Salkhino **$$** *Kronversky Prospect 25; tel. (812) 232 7891*. Great Georgian cooking, but not cheap.

St Petersburg **$$$** *Griboedova Kanal 5; tel. (812) 314 4947*. Russian restaurant in authentic St Petersburg style, with stained glass and a hint of art deco, located opposite the Church of the Saviour on Spilled Blood. A great wine list and good service.

Tandoor **$$** *Voznesenskij Prospekt 2, near St. Isaac's Cathedral; tel. (812) 312 3886*. If you are a vegetable lover, try this Indian restaurant. You will find many choices on their large menu, and the food is delicious.

Tinkoff **$$** *Ulitsa Kazanskaya 7; tel. (812) 118 5566*. Hip club and restaurant. Great salads, pizza and sushi. Impressively, it has its own microbrewery.

Troitsky Most **$** *Malaya Posadksaya Ulitsa 4; Kronvergsky Prospect 29; tel. (812) 232 6693*. The best bargain in town. Fine and original vegetarian cooking.

Zov Ilicha (Lenin's Mating Call) **$$** *Kazanskaya Ulitsa 34; tel. (812) 117 8641*. The interior is a great parody on the Soviet era, but at capitalist prices. Russian and French cuisine.

INDEX